KU-648-484

Contents

Who's Who in D. H. Lawrence

Who's Who
in D. H. Lawrence

GRAHAM HOLDERNESS

ELM TREE BOOKS
HAMISH HAMILTON · LONDON

First published in Great Britain 1976
by Elm Tree Books Ltd
90 Great Russell Street
London WC1

Jacket photograph courtesy of the
Radio Times Hulton Picture Library

The extracts from D. H. Lawrence's work are
reprinted by kind permission of the Estate of the
late Mrs Frieda Lawrence, Laurence Pollinger
Ltd, William Heinemann Ltd, The Viking Press
Inc., and Alfred A. Knopf, Inc.

Printed in Great Britain
by Western Printing Services Ltd, Bristol

Foreword

Who's Who in D. H. Lawrence, by Graham Holderness, is a valuable book for readers of Lawrence, who is now considered one of the most significant writers of this century.

For a man who lived only forty-four and a half years, he was incredibly productive, as the author not only of a prodigious amount of novels and tales, but also of many challenging essays. In the present book Mr. Holderness deals with all the novels as well as the most important novellas and short stories, concentrating on the characters that appear in them. Even those of us who have dealt extensively with Lawrence across the years cannot instantly recall every person in his fiction, or every phrase of every person. The present volume will benefit both seasoned students of Lawrence and readers less familiar with his work.

The book is not a crib for those seeking plot summaries, for it provides no facile synopses; it is, rather, a key to the understanding of the men, women, and children (and, it must be added, the animals) who appear in Lawrence's fiction. Admittedly, one of the vital elements of his writing—those magically presented landscapes of the Nottinghamshire mining country, the Mexican deserts, the bright Mediterranean—cannot be included in a volume such as this, but on the good side Mr. Holderness gives readers something they may now properly see in perspective: the vividness and forcefulness of the people and the animals.

One of the best features of this volume is the way it presents the material, giving it a value far beyond that of a mere directory. Mr. Holderness does assemble the most important factual information about the characters, but he does so in a flavourful Lawrencean way, either paraphrasing Lawrence's main points about their actions and attitudes, or quoting from Lawrence—not exhaustively, but fully enough to give them a Lawrencean vitality. The very juxtaposition helps, for it makes possible a fresh view of Lawrence's people; we can see how wonderfully he knew and could, in the fullest sense, project living creatures on to the page. This *Who's Who in D. H. Lawrence* is both useful and illuminating.

HARRY T. MOORE
Southern Illinois University

A

ALLPORT, MR.: A boarder at the establishment of Siegmund MacNair's widow, Beatrice; tall and broad, thin as a door, with a remarkably small chin; waywardly humorous, sometimes wistful, sometimes petulant, but always gallant. *The Trespasser*

ALLSOP, CASSIE: An old maid, daughter of a prominent 'Chapel family'; in public thin, nipped and wistful-looking, privately tyrannous and exacting. She offers Alvina Houghton advice on terms of equality as a fellow 'old maid'. *The Lost Girl*

ANNABLE, BILLY: A swarthy urchin with a shockingly short shirt, and big black eyes; one of Annable the gamekeeper's brood of 'natural' children. *The White Peacock*

ANNABLE, FRANK: Gamekeeper of the Nethermere estate; a broad, burly, black-faced fellow, with a magnificent physique, great vigour and vitality, and a swarthy, gloomy face; his fine, powerful, menacing form looms through the forest like 'some malicious Pan'. He is a man of one idea: that all civilisation is 'the painted fungus of rottenness'. A thorough materialist, he scorns all religion and mysticism, and his philosophy is: 'Be a good animal, true to your animal instincts.' Pursuing this philosophy he leaves his wife and children to fend for themselves, like a 'bag of ferrets' or a 'bunch of foxes'. In his youth he abandoned his first unfaithful wife Lady Crystabel (his 'white peacock'), and was left with nothing but his brutal and cynical commitment to the life of an animal. He dies violently in a quarry rockfall—possibly an act of vengeance—and is buried in the sleepy valley in an atmosphere of sunshine and eternal forgetfulness. *The White Peacock*

ANNABLE, MRS.: The dilapidated wife of Frank Annable, a woman with fading, frowzy red-brown hair; his mate, and the mother of his swarm of 'natural' children, including Jack, Sarah Anne, and the diabolical Sam, who creates riot and scandal by stealing a pet rabbit for domestic consumption. *The White Peacock*

ANNIE: Maid to the Saxton family. *The White Peacock*

ANTHONY: When the Priestess of Isis is a young girl in Rome, 'the golden Anthony' often sits with her and talks of the philosophies and the gods, in the splendour of his great limbs and glowing manhood. 'Why', he asks her, 'is the flower of you so soft and cool within? A maid should open to the sun, when the sun leans forward to caress her.' And his big, bright eyes laugh down on her, bathing her in a lovely glow of male beauty and amorousness. But she does not open to Anthony: the flower of herself is cold. *The Man who Died*

ANTHONY, ALFRED (ALFY): A Bestwood child, who steals the boy William Morel's veteran 'cobbler' (conker) and has his collar ripped off in reprisal. The incident, and Mrs. Anthony's subsequent complaint, is the occasion of a quarrel in the Morel family, with the mother protecting the boy. *Sons and Lovers*

ANTHONY, MRS.: Mother of Alfy, a black-haired, strange little body, a neighbour of the Morels', who seams stockings in her spare time for twopence-ha'penny a dozen. *Sons and Lovers*

ANTONIO, DON: Kate Leslie's fat landlord; a prominent *Fascista*, held in great esteem by the reactionary Knights of Cortés. *The Plumed Serpent*

APSLEY, MAJOR BASIL: The 'adorable' husband of Lady Daphne Apsley; a tall well-bred Englishman, with a strong, easy body, beautiful and well-fleshed, warm brown hair, and simple, amused blue eyes. In the early days of their marriage, he is to Daphne like Dionysos, full of sap and fertility, milk and honey; together they enjoy a simple and lovely intimacy, in which he gives himself to her with unstinting generosity, 'like an ear of corn for her gathering'. His life seems to her like the light of a white star, brightly and incessantly flowing down to her. Captured in Turkey, Basil is a prisoner for much of the war: and on his return he is 'altered'—Daphne perceives the difference immediately she hears his voice, changed from the 'deliberate, diffident, drawling voice', with its exaggerated Cambridge intonations, to a voice as cold, as hard, as inhuman as cold blue steel. His face is gaunt with a deathly pallor, and a livid wound-scar marks his face—and he himself seems as if disfigured by a scar in his brain. To Daphne, fascinated but repelled, he is like death, risen death. He sees her now as Aphrodite, moon-mother of the world, and worships her with a strange fanaticism; he shrinks with an agony of repulsion from physical contact, yet insatiably desires it. Even after the war, Basil continues to believe in *love* as the great power that draws all human beings together; and although she consciously and rationally agrees with him, Daphne is infinitely more attracted to the ancient, unfathomable knowledge of Count Dionys. As Dionys claims Daphne for his nocturnal bride, Basil's desire for her leaves him, and a pure, abstract, sexless feeling takes its place. Perceiving Dionys' power, Basil gives in; and prays only that life shall spare him any further effort of action. *The Ladybird*

APSLEY, LADY DAPHNE: The daughter of the impoverished aristocrats Earl and Countess Beveridge, and poor herself, she yet marries Basil Apsley, a commoner without any money. She is tall, and beautifully built, with a fine stature and straight shoulders; with soft, heavy hair of a pallid gold ash-blond. But her beauty is a failure, she is ill, always ill: even her lovely fair face, with its delicate pink cheeks, is of a soft, exotic white complexion, artificial like a hothouse flower; her eyes, large, beautiful and green-blue, full, languid, almost glaucous, are sad and reddened, nerve-worn, with heavy, blue-veined lids; her throat is thin and white, and her slow, sonorous voice melancholy, protective and sad. Unlike the perpetual Samaritan her mother, Daphne was not born for philanthropy and grief, for caring and weeping over others' sufferings: she has a strong and reckless nature, a wild energy dammed up inside her. But in her mind she has been brought up to admire the *good*. She needs a wild, reckless, dare-devil as a mate, but in her rational consciousness she hates all dare-devils. So her reckless blood and her energy turn to bitterness, frustrated anger, physical illness; while her will remains fixed in her mother's creed, that life should be good and gentle, charitable and benevolent. But while Lady Beveridge thrives on the war, flourishes in the midst of so

3

much suffering to be relieved, Daphne's hope is killed—the spectacle of so much pain makes her long for the end of the world. But then she is fascinated by a hospitalised German war prisoner, Count Dionys: his strange talk puzzles her, but she begins to be stirred by his words with a curious latency; her conscious mind recoils from his 'esoteric knowledge', but her spirit is deeply moved. Her consciousness is like a great weight of stone, which must be broken before any new influence can be admitted: so that on her husband's return she can force Dionys' influence to 'die out of her'. She awaits her husband in the expectation that he will have been purified and renewed by the terrible fires of suffering: but she finds him instead cold and altered—he freezes her heart with the ecstatic, focused white light of his slave-like passion, his prostrate worship of the Aphrodite in her. She is repelled, but also filled with immense satisfaction and power at this sacrament of supreme worship. After the 'awful outpouring of his adoration lust', she is left in torment; for herself, she is not strong and pure enough, she cannot believe sufficiently in her own woman-godhead to bear such extremities of worship. She cannot stay 'intensified and resplendent, in her white, womanly powers, her female mystery'. When Daphne hears Count Dionys singing to himself in the night, unconsciously uttering his own isolated soul in the darkness, she passes beyond the world, into a peace of forgetfulness. Together in the darkness they are transfigured. Dionys goes away, but the union is absolute. Their lives cannot be one life, in the world's day. But she cherishes in her breast the 'dark treasures of stillness and bliss'—'even when her heart was wrung with the agony of knowing he must go.' *The Ladybird*

ARGYLE, JAMES: A writer, a friend of Franz Dekker (Francis) and Angus Guest, Mephistophelean and permanently tipsy. At some time in the past he has evidently been handsome, with his natural dignity and his clean-shaven, strong square face. But now his face is red and softened and inflamed, his eyes have gone small and wicked under his grey brows. His wit is a kind of 'wicked whimsicality' which is very attractive when levelled against someone else. *Aaron's Rod*

ARTHUR: A good-looking, well-nourished young man, a guest of Sir William Franks at Novara with his wife Sybil. *Aaron's Rod*

ASHBY, THE REVEREND MR.: The rector of Tevershall, a nice man of sixty, full of his duty, but personally reduced to a nonentity by the silent 'you leave me alone!' of the village. To the miners he is 'Mester Ashby', a sort of automatic preaching and praying concern. *Lady Chatterley's Lover*

B

BANCROFT, WILL: A singer, guest of the Tempests' at a High-close party; a corpulent man, with hair rippling rather tawdrily, heavily jewelled fingers, and a mellow tenor voice. *The White Peacock*

BANFORD, JILL: A small, thin, delicate thing with spectacles, nearly thirty years old. With her more robust friend Nellie March, she takes a farm; they have the intention of living by themselves and working it. Banford is the principal investor, since March has no money: Banford's father, a tradesman, gives her the money for a start in life, because he loves her, for the sake of her health, and because it doesn't look as if she will get married. But things don't go too well on the farm: the girls are beset by annoying and time-consuming problems and obstacles. Neither of them believes in living for work alone: they like to relax, to read, or cycle in the evenings, but they are prevented by the obstreperous stupidity and obstinate recalcitrance of their hens. And then there is the farm's own demon, the fox that prowls in from the wood and casually carries off the hens under their very noses. The work is oppressive, and March resents slightly having to bear most of its burden. Despite Banford's warmth and generosity, her strange magnanimity, still in the long solitude they become irritable, tired of one another. Banford, always nervous and delicate, becomes more despondent, March more fretful and angry: they begin to lose hope. Then the young soldier Henry Grenfel appears from nowhere. At first afraid, Banford warms to him: she likes company, likes to gossip, is full of perky interest; and she likes someone to wait on—she feels to him as to a younger brother; all her natural warmth and kindness

5

are gratified by assiduous attention to him, and he luxuriates in her sisterly attention. Sensitive to March's feelings, Banford is aware of the affinity between her and Henry, and she irritably resents the intrusion into their lives. She is offended now by what appears as impudence in Henry; she feels sickened by his too penetrating, excessively hot physical presence. She cannot meet his clear, watchful eyes. Between the other two she is fidgety and fretful, she cannot keep still. She is angered into teasing and sarcasm against March. Plaintive, fretful and cross, she tries to hold on to March: but when Henry informs Banford of their agreement to marry, Banford is deeply wounded, like a shot bird, a poor little sick bird. Once she has got March to herself again Banford expresses all her fears and misgivings, her suspicion, hostility and contempt of the youth, her jealousy. March comforts her, with her soft, deep, tender voice and wonderful gentleness. March agrees that Henry should leave the farm. Although they have agreed to marry, when he returns to his camp Banford claims March again, restoring her former character, encouraging her to reject him. But the boy will not be beaten. He returns, and fulfils the inevitable necessity of his life by killing his rival. Banford falls prey to the ruthless insistence of the hunter, who will not be balked of his deepest instinctive desires. *The Fox*

BANFORD, MR. and MRS.: A little, stout, elderly man, with a pink face, a white beard, and smallish, pale-blue eyes; Jill Banford's father. A well-off tradesman, he provides his daughter with the capital necessary to buy Bailey Farm. His manner towards the two girls is always satirical, ironic, mocking. He is present on the farm, accompanied by his little, stout-faced, rosy wife, when Henry Grenfel performs his summary execution of Banford. *The Fox*

BARKER, ISRAEL: Walter Morel's fellow-butty (a sub-contractor, joint leader of a gang of colliers); a quiet, compact little man, who looks as if he would go through a brick wall. *Sons and Lovers*

BEARDSALL, CYRIL: Wistful, nostalgic, effete and lyrical, Cyril is a vaporous self-image of his creator, D. H. Lawrence. All around him lives blossom into passion and decay into tragedy, but Cyril remains untouched: 'I wished that in all the wild valley, something would call me forth from my rooted loneliness.' *The White Peacock*

BEARDSALL, FRANK: Alias French Carlin, husband of Mrs. Beardsall, father of Cyril and Lettie. Having abandoned his family when the children were babies, he reappears, slovenly and neglected, pale and wan with sickness and dissipation. He conceals his identity and shortly afterwards dies alone, unpitied and unlamented by his family. *The White Peacock*

BEARDSALL, LETTICE (LETTIE): Daughter of Frank and Mrs. Beardsall, sister of Cyril, beloved of George Saxton, affianced and eventually married to Leslie Tempest. She is tall and slenderly formed, her hair yellow, with beautiful eyes and brows. Lithe and firmly moulded, naturally graceful, 'in her poise and harmonious movements are revealed the subtle sympathies of her artist's soul.' She treats her admirer George Saxton with snobbery, teasing, flirtation and insurgent tenderness; she admires his physical beauty, but recoils from his coarse-fibred toughness, his 'commonness' and 'vulgarity'. They experience exquisite moments of intense passion, mingled with a shiver of fear. But Lettie reluctantly chooses the more eligible Leslie Tempest, though he too has his characteristic inadequacies: in the presence of a wood filled with snowdrops, a 'sad and mysterious communion of pure wild things', she feels the yearning for some lost knowledge and understanding that has departed; Leslie's insensitivity to her feelings makes him seem 'unreal' to her. But gradually she submits to him; she folds around them the 'snug curtain of the present', shutting out distant prospects, and only occasionally does she peep out from the shelter into the spaces beyond. Established as a wife and mother, Lettie reaches the point where all things seem worthless and insipid; she is determined to ignore herself, and to live her life at second hand. So she indulges her husband and serves her children; remaining beautiful, brilliant, fascinating, but unfulfilled. *The White Peacock*

BEARDSALL, MRS.: Wife of Frank, mother of Cyril and Lettie. Small, plump and fifty-odd, she had been abandoned by her 'vulgar' and deceiving husband Frank, who left her for 'other pleasures' eighteen years earlier. She lives a quiet, comfortable, cultured existence, preserving wistful memories of the romance that might have been. She coldly disapproves of Cyril's relationship with Emily Saxton. *The White Peacock*

BEEBY, MR.: A lawyer, a little man, all grey, who is engaged in disentangling the disastrous affairs of James Houghton after his death. *The Lost Girl*

BELL: Formerly American manager of the lakeside hotel at Orilla where Kate Leslie stays; he narrowly escaped death when José was murdered by Indians. *The Plumed Serpent*

BELL, MR. A.: Shabbily-dressed, stout, slack and unconcerned friend of Mr. George, the lawyer; with his friend Mr. Swallow, he helps to mystify Jack Grant with his colonial anecdotes, reminiscences and unintelligible Australian humour. *The Boy in the Bush*

BENNERLEY, LADY EVA: An aunt of Clifford Chatterley; a thin woman of sixty, with a red nose; a widow and something of a *grande dame*. She is perfectly simple and frank, and superficially kind. She is not at all a snob—far too sure of herself. She is perfect at the social sport of coolly holding her own, and making other people defer to her. *Lady Chatterley's Lover*

BENTLEY, LORD WILLIAM: Member of Parliament and friend of Mrs. Hardy, the Squire's lady. *The Rainbow*

BENTLEY, MISS: Proprietor of a tea-shop in Uthwaite: a shallow old maid with a rather large nose and a romantic disposition, who serves tea to Lady Chatterley with a careful intensity worthy of a sacrament. *Lady Chatterley's Lover*

BERRY: A brown, shy young man, a guest at Wragby Hall, who makes stupid and inconsequential contributions to the conversation. *Lady Chatterley's Lover*

BETTS, MRS.: Housekeeper at Wragby Hall. *Lady Chatterley's Lover*

BEVERIDGE, COUNTESS: Wife of Earl Beveridge and mother of Lady Daphne; she is a frail, bird-like woman with a long, pale, wan face, elegant, but with an unmistakeable touch of the bluestocking. In her capacious heart of pity and kindness, she loves humanity, especially her enemies. Her life is in her sorrows, and in her efforts on behalf of the sufferings of others. She is generally regarded as 'the soul of England', and exerts a strong influence over leading political figures by the power of her 'pure fragrance of truth and love'. This little, unyielding Mater Dolorosa, agonised by the deaths of her own sons in the war, visits with benevolence and charitable solicitude the wounded German officers in hospital, and there encounters Count Dionys, whom she introduces to Lady Daphne. Towards the end of the war she begins to lose some of her influence and power, as a new generation begins to sneer at the outdated drawing-room of this shabby, old-fashioned aristocrat. *The Ladybird*

BEVERIDGE, EARL: Father of Lady Daphne, a handsome, proud, brutal man, descended from a desperate race of dare-devil border soldiers. With his dark, sombre face, that would have been haughty if haughtiness had not made it rather ridiculous, he is a passionate man, with a passionate man's sensitiveness, generosity and instinctive overbearing. But his nature, repudiated and labelled as selfish, sensual and cruel by conventional morality, is repressed into saturnine sullenness. He is defensive and reserved to Count Dionys, whose own haughtiness irritates him; but despite himself, he is forced to respect the courtesy, the aristocratic breeding and the indefinable power of the strange little man who is to be Lady Daphne's lover. *The Ladybird*

BILL: A labourer working on Mr. Wookey's farm. *Love Among the Haystacks*

BILL: An ugly, wizened old serving-man at the Ram Inn. *The White Peacock*

BINGHAM, LADY PRIMROSE: Sister to Major Basil Apsley; not a bit like a primrose, but long-faced, clever and smart. *The Ladybird*

BIRKIN, RUPERT: Pale and ill-looking, with a narrow but nicely made figure; when dressed correctly, there is an innate incongruity which causes a slight ridiculousness in his appearance. His nature is unconventional, clever and separate. Ursula Brangwen is struck by a basic contradiction in him— there is on the one hand a wonderful, attractive flow and

9

rapidity of life, a curious hidden richness in him, the rare quality of an utterly desirable man; and on the other hand, a ridiculous, mean, self-effacement into a Saviour and a Sunday School teacher, 'a prig of the stiffest type'. Birkin is completely disillusioned by his world and its ideals: he no longer believes in humanity, no longer cares a straw for the social ideals he lives by, would like to 'absolutely smash up the old idols' to clear a way for the growth of something new. So he leaves his job as a School Inspector, abandoning his educational work. He loves Ursula and wants union with her, but he does not want the old concept of love, and especially not the stifling, suffocating intimacy of conventional marriage. He offers Ursula not love, but a meeting of absolute impersonal selves, of stark, unknown beings, utterly strange creatures—'a strange conjunction, not meeting and mingling, but an equilibrium, a pure balance of two single beings, as the stars balance each other.' Rejecting both love and sensuality, Birkin strives in his marriage with Ursula to achieve 'the paradisal entry into pure, single being'—where the individual soul is more important than love or desire for union, existing in a lovely state of 'free, proud singleness', accepting the responsibility of permanent connections with others, but never forfeiting its individual singleness. He is confronted too with the problem of love and eternal conjunction between men: it is also necessary to love a man purely and fully. He offers Gerald Crich such a relationship, a blood-brotherhood, but Gerald fails him—in death the frozen body of the other man denies Birkin's love with the terrible look of cold, mute matter. But Birkin perversely and heroically continues to believe that another love than that of man for woman is both necessary and possible. *Women in Love*

BLESSINGTON, BOYD: A tall, thin, rather hollow-chested man, with a black beard and eyeglasses. A widower with five children, he is regarded as an eminently presentable suitor for Mary Rath. He loves her with a real, though rather *social* love, uneasy and desirous. A nice man, rather frail and sad; belonging absolutely to the social world, he sees nothing outside it. *The Boy in the Bush*

BLESSINGTON, HILDA: A thin, nervous girl, daughter of Boyd Blessington, with dark-grey, startled eyes. *The Boy in the Bush*

BLOGG, UNCLE: Methodist son-in-law of Jacob Ellis, husband of Ruth; who prays for the dying Grandmother, and accompanies her to the grave with hymns sung in a fat, wheezy Methodist voice. *The Boy in the Bush*

BOB, OLD: Barman at the Royal Oak. *Aaron's Rod*

BOLTON, IVY: A nurse employed to attend to Sir Clifford Chatterley: a rather good-looking woman of forty-odd, attentive and polite, speaking in heavily correct English, but with a broad slur. From having bossed the sick colliers for many years, she has a fair amount of confidence and assurance, and a very good opinion of herself. Ever since her collier husband Ted was killed in an underground explosion, Ivy has borne a deep grudge against the ruling class of 'masters'; and yet she feels superior to the colliers, her own people. She is thrilled by her contact with Clifford, a man of the upper class; she feels herself coming into possession, bit by bit, of all the gentry's knowledge, of everything that makes them upper-class. Gradually she achieves a kind of power over Clifford, doing everything for him; at first he resents the 'infinitely soft touch' of her fingers on his face, shaving him; but then he begins to like it, with a growing voluptuousness. 'Gradually, with infinite softness, she was getting him by the throat, and he was yielding to her.' When Connie leaves Clifford for Mellors, he lapses back into a childish submission to Mrs. Bolton's power, gazing on her with wide, childish eyes, in a 'relaxation of madonna worship'. She is both thrilled and ashamed: she is the Magna Mater, full of power and potency, subjecting the great man-child to the domination of her will. *Lady Chatterley's Lover*

BOSWELL, JOE: 'The Gipsy'—one of the black, loose-bodied, handsome sort, with a loose pose, a gaze insolent in its indifference, a thin black moustache under his thin straight nose, and a big silk handkerchief of yellow and red round his neck. A beau in his way, handsome and curiously elegant, and quite expensive in his gipsy fashion. He singles out Yvette from her nondescript companions, fascinated and drawn by the tender mystery of her virginity—'like a mysterious early flower, like a snowdrop in the waking sleep of its brief blossoming.' When the flooded River Papple destroys the Rectory, the monolithic

Granny, and the whole sordid structure of Yvette's intolerable life, the gipsy saves her, cherishing her with his naked body, sustaining life within her; then silently, invisibly, departs. *The Virgin and the Gipsy*

BOSWELL, MRS.: Joe Boswell the gipsy's wife; a dark-faced woman, with a pink shawl round her head and gold earrings; handsome in a bold, dark-faced wolfish way. *The Virgin and the Gipsy*

BOWER, MRS.: A neighbour of the Morels', fat and waddling, who bosses the house during Mrs. Morel's labour. There is no end to her sharp disgust with the ways of men. *Sons and Lovers*

BRADLEY, MISS: Young, athletic-looking guest of Hermione Roddice at Breadalby; enthusiastically fit and healthy, she earns Gudrun Brangwen's 'silent loathing'. *Women in Love*

BRAITHWAITE: A farmer, acquaintance of Tom Brangwen, who teases his stepdaughter Anna. *The Rainbow*

BRAITHWAITE, MR.: Chief cashier at the colliery, and an important shareholder in the firm. He pays out the miners' wages, to the accompaniment of patriarchal admonitions. *Sons and Lovers*

BRANGWEN, ALFRED (SENIOR): Head of the Brangwen household in the 1840s. With a humorous puckering at the eyes, a sort of fat laugh, very quiet and full, he is spoilt like a lord of creation. *The Rainbow*

BRANGWEN, ALFRED (JUNIOR): Son of Alfred (Senior), a draughtsman in a lace-factory in Nottingham. He is rather heavy and uncouth, with a broad Derbyshire accent, sticking tenaciously to his work and his town position, becoming fairly well-off. But at a price: at drawing his instinct is towards big, bold lines, rather lax, so it is a cruel discipline for him to 'pedgill away at the lace-designing, working from the tiny squares of his paper, counting and plotting and niggling'. But he persists stubbornly, crushing his instinctive self. He marries the daughter of a chemist, a woman of social pretensions, and becomes something of a snob. Later he turns after 'forbidden pleasures', a silent, inscrutable follower of his own desires,

'neglecting his indignant bourgeois wife without a qualm'.
The Rainbow

BRANGWEN, ALICE: Elder daughter of Alfred (Senior), she marries a collier and lives stormily for a time in Ilkeston, before moving away to Yorkshire with her numerous young family. *The Rainbow*

BRANGWEN, ANNA: Formerly Lensky, daughter of Lydia and Paul Lensky, stepdaughter of Tom Brangwen. She is a child with a face like a bud of apple-blossom, and glistening fair hair like thistledown sticking out in straight, wild, flamey pieces, and very dark eyes. An independent, forgetful little soul, with a passion for eminence and dominance, she bears some of the burden of the marital difficulties of her parents: until Tom and Lydia achieve the transfiguration of a fulfilled relationship, and Anna's soul becomes at peace between them. She is no longer called upon to uphold with her childish might 'the broken end of the arch'; 'her father and mother now met to the span of the heavens, and she, the child, was free to play in the space beneath, between'. As a girl, Anna has a curious contempt for ordinary people, a benevolent superiority, mistrusting intimacy, hating people who come too near to her. It is only her cousin Will Brangwen who represents to her the possibility of transgressing the bounds of her experience: he is 'the hole in the wall, beyond which the sunshine blazed on an outside world'. After their marriage, Will and Anna find themselves spiritually alone and isolated, 'the only inhabitants of the visible earth', a law unto themselves. They are like the centre of a great wheel which is the outside world: the rim of the wheel spins on in motion and activity, but at the centre is a poised, unflawed stillness, beyond time. But soon the 'recurrence of love and conflict' begins between them. Anna wants stability, an inner surety, a confidence in the abidingness of his love; but she does not get it. Will's most intense experiences are his moments of dark emotional communion with the Church, its emblems, symbols and its art, such as his ecstasy in Lincoln Cathedral. Anna resents these experiences, and tries to destroy them in him by mocking and ridiculing the Church—she is a rationalist who believes in the omnipotence of the human mind, clings to the worship of human knowledge. Will feels she is jeering at his very soul. Ultimately their relationship does not unfold or develop, does not *go* anywhere, though they do discover a kind of impersonal fulfilment in pure sensuality. After Ursula is born, Anna decides that there is no necessity to travel any further into experience. She lapses into the vague content of fecund, teeming, incessantly productive matriarchy: 'Through her another soul was coming, to stand upon her as upon the thereshold, looking out, shading its eyes for the direction to take.' *The Rainbow*, *Women in Love*

BRANGWEN, CATHERINE: Daughter of Will and Anna Brangwen. *The Rainbow*

BRANGWEN, DORA: One of the younger daughters of Will and Anna Brangwen. *Women in Love*

BRANGWEN, EFFIE: Younger daughter of Alfred (Senior). *The Rainbow*

BRANGWEN, FRANK: Third son of Alfred (Senior): a handsome lad with soft brown hair and regular features, easily excitable and carried away, weak in character. As a child he is attracted to the slaughterhouse by the trickle of dark blood running across the pavement; later he takes over the butchery business, but is neglectful of it through a certain callousness and contempt. He drinks, and is often in his public house blathering away as if he knows everything—when in reality he is recognised as a noisy fool. *The Rainbow*

BRANGWEN, FRED: Son of Tom (Senior) and Lydia Brangwen; a real Brangwen, large-boned, blue-eyed and very English. He is his father's very son, and after his death succeeds to the farm. He is sensitive and fond of reading; like all the Brangwens, very much a thing to himself, though fond of people and indulgent to them. But Fred is restless and discontented: he wants something, love, passion, and he cannot find them. Eventually he marries Laura, a handsome girl fresh out of Salisbury Training College. *The Rainbow*

BRANGWEN, GUDRUN: As a child, with her long, sleepy body and endless chain of fancies, Gudrun will have nothing to do with realities. It is no good trying to make her responsible: she floats along like a fish in the sea, perfect within the medium of her own being. At twenty-five years old, a sculptress and

teacher of art, she is very beautiful, soft-skinned and soft-limbed, 'charming in her softness and her fine, exquisite richness of texture and delicacy of line'. There is also about her something playful and ironical, a piquancy, a separateness and an untouched reserve. Seeing Gerald Crich, she is overwhelmed by a paroxysm, a violent transport of sensations, and realises that in some way she is singled out for him—there is a 'pale, gold, arctic light' that envelops only the two of them; and when she witnesses Gerald forcing his mare to face the passing train, she is numbed by the sense of sheer power and pure will: 'the indomitable, soft weight of the man, clenching the palpitating body of the horse into pure control'. Gudrun hates the industrial environment of Beldover, and yet finds in it a 'foul kind of beauty'; the heavy, gold glamour of the atmosphere seems to envelop her in a labourer's caress, the air is surcharged with a resonance of physical men, a glamorous thickness of labour and maleness. Finally there is between Gudrun and Gerald a 'hellish recognition' of kinship—they are initiated into obscene rites, implicated in abhorrent mysteries; Gudrun feels a subterranean desire to let go, to fling away everything and to lapse into sheer unrestraint, brutal and licentious. When Gerald comes to her after his father's death, she restores him in her enveloping soft warmth, her 'wonderful creative heat'; and he worships her as 'the great bath of life'. But she is 'destroyed into consciousness' by their union, left behind and separate. Looking at his sleeping face, he seems to her beautiful and far-off, perfected: 'They would never be together. Ah, this awful inhuman distance which would always be interposed between her and another being.' A deep resolve forms in her, to combat Gerald: in the corrosive destructiveness of their passion, one of them must triumph over the other. And ultimately it is Gerald who cannot live the experience through to its conclusion: he fails to kill Gudrun, and dies himself, leaving her cold, impassive, unmoved by the frozen, 'barren' tragedy.
The Rainbow, Women in Love

BRANGWEN, LYDIA: Formerly Lensky; wife of Tom Brangwen (Senior), mother of Anna, Tom, Fred; widow of Paul Lensky, Polish intellectual and patriot. She is small and slight, her face pale and clear; she has thick dark eyebrows and a wide mouth, and wide, grey-brown eyes with very dark, fathomless pupils. After her first husband's death she is alone in England with her child Anna: knowing nothing of English life, she walks isolated among the cold, slightly hostile host of English people—until she meets Tom Brangwen, and feels immediately 'the rooted safety of him, and the life in him'. After her marriage to Tom she remains strange and foreign, in some ways removed from him; in her pregnancy she withdraws into herself, leaving him isolated and alone; he feels like 'a broken arch, thrust sickeningly out for support . . . her response was gone, he thrust at nothing.' But she is undoubtedly and absolutely his wife: in the agony of her labour, she looks at him 'as a woman in childbirth looks at the man who begot the child in her; in the extreme hour, an impersonal look, female to male.' *The Rainbow*

BRANGWEN, ROSALIND: One of the younger daughters of Will and Anna Brangwen. *Women in Love*

BRANGWEN, THERESA: Third daughter of Will and Anna Brangwen, sister of Ursula, and Gudrun, Catherine, William and Cassandra. A great, strapping, bold hussy, who remains at home when the elder sisters go away to college, 'indifferent to all higher claims'. *The Rainbow*

BRANGWEN, TOM (SENIOR): Son of Alfred, brother of Alfred, Frank, Alice and Effie; the youngest son, and his mother's favourite. As a child he was sent forcibly to Grammar School, where he proved an 'unwilling failure', unable to fulfil his mother's ambitions by being 'clever' and becoming a gentleman. Emotionally he is highly developed, sensitive and delicate, refined in instinct; in mental things a fool. He is glad therefore to get back to the farm—'I have got a turnip on my shoulders, let me stick to th' fallow.' For a time his life as a farmer suffices him; he has youth and vigour, humour and a comic wit, and the will and power to forget his own shortcomings. But as a young man he is filled with unsatisfied yearnings for he knows not what, inarticulate desires which he assuages with brandy—until he meets Lydia Lensky, and instantly recognises the door to his own fulfilment: 'That's her!' He finds himself suddenly in the world beyond reality, as if a new creation were fulfilled: 'And then it came upon him that he would marry her, and she would be his life.' Their marriage is by no means easy: but after long and often bitter struggles they achieve in their relationship the consummation, the fulfilment, the baptism to another life, the complete confirmation. 'They had passed through the doorway into the further space . . . it was the transfiguration, the glorification, the admission.' A patriarch of the old pre-industrial world, Tom is drowned by the great flood which ushers in the future. *The Rainbow*

BRANGWEN, TOM (JUNIOR): Son of Tom and Lydia Brangwen. As a young man short and good-looking, with crisp black hair and long black eyelashes, and soft, dark, possessed eyes. He has a quick intelligence, and an instinct for attracting people of character and energy. But Tom only exists through other people; alone, he is unresolved, and his dark eyes betray a deep misery 'which he wears with the same ease and pleasantness as he wears his close-fitting clothes'. He is a gentleman, yet undefinably an outsider, belonging to nowhere, to no society. Later during Ursula Brangwen's adolescence, we find Tom at the end of his desires, having done everything he wanted to do, and having arrived at a 'stability of nullification', a 'disintegrated lifelessness of soul'. He is content to preserve intact the empty shell of his life, as he is content to acquiesce in the meaningless existence of the Wiggiston colliers. When he meets the lesbian Winifred Inger, he detects in her 'a kinship with his own dark corruption'; and they marry to share the putrescent spiritual corruption of their empty lives. *The Rainbow*

BRANGWEN, URSULA: Even as a girl of twelve, Ursula wants to burst the narrow bounds of the little town of Cossethay, where only limited people live. She yearns for the world beyond, where all is vastness, and 'throngs of real, proud people' whom she could love. In imagination she lives an intensely passionate experience of religion, in which her ideal of a man figures as one of the 'Sons of God, who took to wife the daughters of men'. As she passes from girlhood to womanhood, she finds the cloud of self-responsibility gathering upon her. She resents the necessity of growing up, the 'heavy, numbing responsibility of living an undiscovered life'; she has no sense of direction, knows not where to go or how to become herself;

she craves only for the breast of the Son of Man, to lie there. Anton Skrebensky brings to her a sense of the outer world beyond, as if she could feel the whole world lying spread before her; but when Skrebensky describes his personal identification with the 'nation', and expresses his individual life as a mere function within a social mechanism, he seems like 'nothing' to her. Their relationship becomes a locked tension of wills, 'his will set and straining with all its tension to encompass and compel her; and her will set against his'. But besides Skrebensky, there is for Ursula another discovery—there is the mysterious 'man's world' to be ventured on, the world of work and duty, which she aspires to conquer. But teaching at the raw and ugly Brinsley Street school, she finds herself a prisoner of the industrial world; to teach effectively she must cease to be her personal self, and become Ursula Brangwen, Standard Five Teacher. There is no escape: she must brutally thrash the insolent and rebellious children to impose order, and this represents a great violation of her soul. The University College too is discovered to be a mere department of the industrial machine; a little, slovenly laboratory for the factory. So with Rupert Birkin she abandons her job and leaves all her past behind, in a final 'transit out of life'; leaving England, the child she had been, playing in Cossethay churchyard, seems a little creature of history, not really herself. She wants to have no past: she wants 'to have come down from the slopes of heaven' with Birkin. And it is in Birkin that she discovers an experience more wonderful than life itself: 'the strange mystery of his life motion, at the back of his thighs'. It is there she discovers him one of the Sons of God, such as were in the beginning of the world; not a man, something other, something more. Their feelings are neither love nor passion; the experience is infinite and impersonal—it is the daughters of men coming back to the sons of God. *The Rainbow, Women in Love*

BRANGWEN, WILLIAM (WILL): Son of Alfred (Junior); draughtsman in a lace factory in Nottingham, Will enters the Marsh Farm like some mysterious animal that lived in the darkness under the leaves and never came out; a long, thin youth, with hair like sleek, thin fur, with a bright face, and among all his shyness a self-possession, an unawareness of what others might be, since he was himself. He finds himself, to his wonder, in 'an electric state of passion' for Anna, his heart fierce and insistent with desire. In their passionate avowal of love, he feels the hand of the hidden Almighty thrusting out of the darkness and gripping him; he goes his way 'subject and in fear, his heart gripped and burning from the touch'. His decision to marry Anna is fixed and unalterable, and he resists all the difficulties and obstacles created by the Brangwens. Will is mindless, instinctive, craving for some dark, nameless emotion, the mystery of passion. He hardly cares about himself as a human being, hardly attaches any importance to his social life or his work; his real being lies in 'the dark emotional experience of the Infinite, the Absolute'. He fulfils these emotions in his relationship with the Church, as in his mystical ecstasy in Lincoln Cathedral; and in his relations with Anna—though she resists and struggles against the great strain of his inordinate desires. Gradually their marriage becomes a battle, a locked tension of wills; but the recurrence of conflict between them is interspersed with moments of supremely beautiful intimacy and communion, the tremulous wonder of consummation. But still Will is unsatisfied, he rages in torment, wanting, wanting, 'his soul a black torment of unfulfilment'. The only solution to their struggle is discovered in a complete abandoning of external responsibilities and moral pressures, their decision to seek in each other 'gratification, pure and simple'. There is no love or tenderness between them; only 'the maddening, sensuous lust for discovery and the insatiable, exorbitant gratification in the sensual beauties of her body'. Their love becomes a sensuality as violent and extreme as death. But from this sensuality Will at last develops a social identity, a 'real, purposive self', which is realised in his educational activity as a Handwork Instructor; and from his connection with the great human endeavour, he gains a new vigour. *The Rainbow, Women in Love*

BRANGWEN, WILLIAM (BILLY): Son of Will and Anna; a lovable, delicate child. *The Rainbow, Women in Love*

BREDON, MR.: Formerly a groom and jockey, now a tramp: a very seedy, slinking fellow with a tang of horsey braggadocio about him. He is small, thin and ferrety, with a week's red beard bristling on his pointed chin. He comes slouching into the hayfield of the Wookeys' farm, asking for work. They offer him food, which he eats greedily, in a debased and parasitic fashion which disgusts the farmers. He is followed unrelentingly by his wife Lydia, who will not leave him although she finds her relation to him bitterly humiliating and degrading. *Love Among the Haystacks*

BREDON, LYDIA: Wife of the tramp Mr. Bredon. She is small and finely made; her face is small, ruddy and comely, except for a look of bitterness and aloofness. Her hair drawn tightly back, she gives an impression of cleanness, of precision, of directness. Quite young, she would be pretty if she were not hard, embittered and callous-looking. As she speaks angrily and contemptuously to her husband, Geoffrey Wookey feels a certain kinship with her—they are both at odds with the world. Towards her husband's slouching, parasitic insolence, he feels only loathing, and longs to exterminate him. Lydia encounters Geoffrey again in the hayfield at night, as she looks for her husband; seeking him more out of necessity and stubborn vindictiveness than out of any attachment or affection. She is determined that he is not going to 'have it his own road'. As Geoffrey warms and comforts her, her bitter disillusionment with life, the unalleviated shame and degradation of her recent years, her loneliness, hardness and sterility, all melt into softening tears, and she clings to Geoffrey in a little frenzy of pain. Geoffrey wants to marry her; but she feels a natural and justified suspicion of men and their intentions. She will wait for him, if he really does want her; though she feels he is more likely to change his mind. But Geoffrey and Lydia keep faith with one another. *Love Among the Haystacks*

BREWITT: A big, fine, good-humoured collier, one of the 'superior type' of miners who gather for intellectual discussion in the Royal Oak. *Aaron's Rod*

BRICKNELL, ALFRED: Father of Julia (Mrs. Robert Cunningham) and Jim, a partner in the colliery firm; his English is incorrect, his accent broad Derbyshire, and he is not a gentleman—yet he is well-to-do, and very stuck-up. *Aaron's Rod*

BRICKNELL, JIM: A tall, big fellow of thirty-eight, his young forehead bald, and raised in odd wrinkles; a silent half-grin on his face, a little tipsy, a little satyr-like. He is a socialist, a 'red-hot revolutionary of a very ineffectual sort', and hence he patronises the ex-miner and itinerant flautist Aaron Sisson. Jim wants to be loved—is 'dying for lack of love'; his one desire is to sacrifice himself to the abstract principle of love. *Aaron's Rod*

BROWNING, MRS. CLARISS: A frail, elegant woman, fashionable rather than Bohemian; but a frequenter of the Bricknells' Bohemian set. She is Irish, cream and auburn, with a slightly lifted upper lip that gives her a pathetic look. *Aaron's Rod*

BRUNT, MR.: Assistant teacher at Brinsley Street school; thin, greenish, with a long nose and sharp face. Jolty, jerky and bossy, he teaches like a machine, in a hard, high, inhuman voice. *The Rainbow*

BURLAP, JUDGE: A guest of Mrs. Norris at Tlacolula: a bad-tempered and bad-mannered old man, in a black morning coat, white hair and beard. His normal state is one of 'intense, though suppressed irritation, amounting almost to rabies'. He is filled with irritable hate and frustrated anger with all things Mexican—the country, the people, the President; and all things socialist—the Labour Party, Bolshevism, the Soviet Union. *The Plumed Serpent*

BURLAP, MRS.: Judge Burlap's wife, a woman in black crêpe-de-Chine, with the inevitable baby face and blue eyes and Middle-West accent. 'Impertinent' Kate Leslie concludes: 'a common-place little woman'. *The Plumed Serpent*

BURYAN, JOHN THOMAS: Cornish farmer, who with his sister Ann befriends Richard Lovat Somers. *Kangaroo*

BYRNE, CECIL: After the death of Helena Verden's lover Siegmund, Cecil offers to rouse her and reawaken her to life with his passionate ways; weary and helpless, she is prepared to accept from him at least 'rest and warmth'. *The Trespasser*

C

CALIFANO, GIUSEPPE: Cicio's cousin, husband of Gemma, a *restaurateur* and a flourishing London Italian; a real London product, with the English virtues of cleanliness and honesty added to an Italian shrewdness. He has four children, of whom he is very proud. *The Lost Girl*

CALLADINE, MR.: Caretaker in Woodhouse Chapel. *The Lost Girl*

CALLCOTT, JACK: Foreman in a motor works in Sydney, and neighbour of Richard and Harriet Somers. He is an active and prominent member of the Diggers, the para-military political organisation led by Kangaroo; in Jack's rather long, clean-shaven face, his glowing, smiling eyes have something desirous, and perhaps something fanatical in them. He is handsome in a colonial way, with heavy limbs and well-built; the only delicate part of him being his long pallid face, which seems inappropriate to his strong animal body. There is a dark, lingering look in his eyes, reminding one of 'a patient, enduring animal with an indomitable but naturally passive courage'. He offers Richard Somers personal comradeship and involvement in the Digger movement; and between them exists a feeling of friendship—'a rich, full peace, as if one blood ran warm and rich between them'. But finally Somers rejects Jack's proffered relationship and recoils back on to his isolated individual self. Jack's 'fanaticism' emerges when the Diggers disrupt a socialist meeting, and Jack murders three people—'there's nothing bucks you up like killing a man. You feel a perfect *angel* afterwards.' *Kangaroo*

CALLCOTT, VICTORIA: Wife of Jack Callcott; a very good-looking young woman, with loose brown hair, quick, bright, shy brown eyes, and a warm complexion; 'a delicate, frail face that reminded one of a flickering butterfly in its wavering'. She befriends Harriet, and is attracted to Richard Somers— would like to become his lover; but he lets the moment pass, shies away from the connection. Vickie can be a 'terribly venomous little cat' when she unsheathes her claws; but as long as they remain sheathed, and 'her paws quite velvety and pretty, she remains winsome and charming'. *Kangaroo*

CAPTAIN, THE: A tall man of about forty, a Prussian aristocrat and officer, haughty and overbearing; with a fine, handsomely knit figure, reddish-brown hair, grey at the temples, stiff and cropped close to the skull. With a moustache also cropped short, bristling over a full, brutal mouth; and fair eyebrows standing bushy over light blue eyes, always flashing and dancing with a cold fire. The deep lines in his rugged, thin-cheeked face, and the irritable tension of his brow give him the look of a man who has to fight with life, and with himself. The Captain is unmarried, and no woman has ever moved him to desire marriage. Occasionally he indulges himself with a mistress or prostitute, but after such an event he returns to his duty even more tense-browed, even more hostile and irritable. To most of the men in his command he is aloof and impersonal, though a devil when roused to anger; they accept him as a matter of course, without feeling any great hostility or aversion. To his orderly he is also at first merely cold and indifferent, an impersonal figure of authority; but gradually, almost unconsciously, he becomes aware of the servant's young, vigorous presence around him. The young man's constant, inescapable presence plays like a warm flame on the older man's tense, rigid body, which is fixed and almost unliving in the mould of discipline, duty, and rigid self-control. The young soldier's warm, physical being pene-trates into the officer's stiffened discipline; but the Captain is a gentleman, with long, fine hands and cultivated move-ments, and he resists the latent stirring of his innate self, his suppressed but passionate nature—is he to be awakened to life by a mere servant? Yet he hates the private's fine black brows, and the free movement of the handsome limbs, which no military discipline can make stiff. He cannot leave the younger man alone: constantly he watches him, gives him sharp orders, taunts him with satire and contempt, becomes harsh and cruelly bullying. But still he does not recognise the passion for what it is, believing he is merely reacting to the obtuseness, clumsiness and stupidity of a perverse and obsti-nate servant. Finally, in a gratification of his deeper instincts, he lashes the orderly in the face with a belt, and feels a thrill of deep pleasure and of shame. To avoid the issue, he takes a woman, to regain his composure; but returns in an agony of irritation, torment and misery. Brutally he assaults the ser-vant, kicking him without mercy, and the experience provides an intense gratification of his passions. But there is also a horrible counter-action, a sense of dissolution and breaking-down. Still by sheer effort of will he prevents himself from

recognising the reality of his feelings, suppressing the knowledge along with his instincts and desires. Ultimately the young man is moved to a torment of anger against the Captain, and consummates his hate in a brutally intimate murder. Hideous in violent death, the Captain's body yet moves the youth to pity—the long, military body represents more than the thing that had bullied and kicked him. It seems a pity that *it* had to be broken. *The Prussian Officer*

CARLIN, FRENCH: *see* Beardsall, Frank

CARLOTA, DOÑA: Wife of Don Ramón Carrasco. A thin, gentle, wide-eyed woman, with a pale, faded face and a slightly startled expression. She is 'delicate and sensitive like a Chihuaha dog, and with the same prominent eyes'. An intense, almost exalted Catholic, she is fiercely opposed to Don Ramón's revival of the pagan rituals of Quetzalcoatl, considering that it amounts to 'mortal sin'. Though their marriage had begun with love, when Ramón had to make the 'great change', to cast his emotional self—which she loved—into the furnace, to be smelted into a new self, she could not follow him. She continues to meet Ramón and the world with Christian love and charity, while he develops spiritually towards the new world of the old gods. So her love becomes, not the spontaneous flow of life, but the exercise of pure despotic *will*. In the midst of a ritual of Quetzalcoatl, conducted in the desecrated church by Don Ramón, she flings herself on to the altar, crying to the banished gods Jesus and Mary, pleading for death and forgiveness for her erring husband. Ramón watches her convulsions of hysterical passion with detached abstraction: there is no connection between them. She dies to the sound of the drums and hymns of Quetzalcoatl, the sounds of men exulting in the power of life; she dies beneath a bitterly vindictive tirade of accusations from Cipriano; and beneath the cruel impassivity of her husband's indifference. 'It is life', he said, 'which is the mystery. Death is hardly mysterious in comparison.' *The Plumed Serpent*

CARRASCO, DON RAMÓN: A wealthy estate owner, a tall, big, handsome man, middle-aged, with a large black moustache and large, rather haughty eyes. Husband to Doña Carlota, and shortly after her death, to Teresa. Don Ramón is dedicated to the cause of the religion of Quetzalcoatl, determined to restore the old pre-Christian faith, ceremonies and rituals to Mexico, as the only means of 'saving' the country from soul-despair and spiritual death. Initially he appears simply as a priest and leader of the cult—'the first man of Quetzalcoatl' —conducting ceremonials and writing hymns, manufacturing cult-objects and distributing propaganda. Later he declares himself to *be* Quetzalcoatl, risen in the flesh. Don Ramón opposes Christ, and the white anti-Christ of charity, and socialism, and politics and reform, which will not save Mexico, but will destroy it. Only in the old faith will men and women be able to rediscover their true manhood and womanhood. As a culmination to his assumption of godhead, Ramón removes the Christian images from the church at Sayula and burns them; then ceremonially establishes in the church the images and cult-objects, the services and rituals, proper to the worship of Quetzalcoatl. *The Plumed Serpent*

CARRINGTON, SIR HENRY: *see* Rico

CARRINGTON, LADY (LOUISE, LOU): Née Witt; an American, of a moderately rich Louisiana family; not exactly pretty, but very attractive, with her 'odd little *museau*'; her clusters of dark, curly New Orleans hair, and her quaint brown eyes that don't quite match—'a bit sleepy and vague, but quick as a squirrel's'. Lou plays at being well-bred, and there is about her a lurking sense of being an outsider everywhere, like a gipsy, belonging everywhere and nowhere—'all this made up her charm and her failure. She didn't quite belong.' Married to Sir Henry Carrington (Rico), Lou is bound to him by a 'nervous attachment', a sexless and passionless 'vibration of nerves'; their relationship is a tension of wills. But Lou only begins to appreciate fully Rico's 'powerlessness', and the meaninglessness of her own life, when she encounters the stallion St. Mawr: 'when dimly, into her weary young woman's soul, an ancient understanding seemed to flood in.' When she sees the dark, passionate blaze of power and of different life in the eyes of the horse, the anxious powerlessness of the man 'drives her mad'; she realises that in Rico everything is a pose, an attitude, whereas 'the black, fiery flow in the eyes of the horse was something much more terrifying and

25

real, the only thing that was real.' Gradually Lou is overcome with a sense of bitterness, of the complete futility of her living—since she has apprehended St. Mawr's terrible 'being', she can hardly believe the world she lives in. After Rico has overturned St. Mawr in the accident, Lou experiences a 'vision of evil', which reveals to her that the whole natural direction of life has been reversed, like the horse, thrown backwards. Her conclusion is that the individual must depart from the mass, and cleanse himself; retreat to the desert, and fight. When St. Mawr's life and virility are threatened, Lou flees to America with her mother Mrs. Witt, and the two grooms, Phoenix and Lewis. Continuing her quest for some reality of experience—'what under heaven was *real*?'—she discovers a ranch in the Rocky Mountains, where she can be alone, free from the bruising entanglements with other people, free to give herself to the other, unseen presences, the 'beauty and naturalness of the living landscape'. She has had enough of people. 'There's something else for me. It's a spirit, and it's here on this ranch. The spirit is wild, and it has waited for me. Now I've come. Now I'm here.' *St. Mawr*

CARTWRIGHT: An artist, friend of Rico. A man of thirty-eight, poor, just beginning to accept himself as a failure. After knocking about Paris and London and Munich, he is trying to become staid, and to persuade himself that English village life, with squire and dean in the background, humble artist in the middle, and labourer in the common foreground, is 'genuine life'. He bears a physical resemblance to Pan, which gives rise to some dinner-table joviality and not a little symbolism. *St. Mawr*

CHARLESWORTH, ALFRED: Colliery manager. He is uneducated, but tries to speak good English in a fat squeaky voice. Walter Morel mocks his authority and is victimised in consequence: Alfred 'did not forgive' him, and ensures that the butty gets poor contracts and bad 'stalls'. *Sons and Lovers*

CHATTERLEY, SIR CLIFFORD: The young baronet, recently married to Constance Reid, is crippled and paralysed by a war wound in 1917. The injuries to the body create corresponding injuries to the soul: 'he had been hurt so much that something inside him had perished.' Some of his feelings have gone: there is a blank of insentience. He has suffered so much that the capacity for suffering has almost left him: he remains strange and bright and cheerful, with his ruddy, healthy face, and his pale-blue, challenging bright eyes. But in his face there is 'the watchful look, the slight vacancy of a cripple'. His very quiet, hesitating voice, his eyes at the same time bold and frightened, assured and uncertain, reveal his nature. His manner is often modest and self-effacing, almost tremulous, and then offensively supercilious. Apart from his sexual impotence, Clifford is incapable of warm, living relationships with other people. An aristocrat and coal-mine owner, he believes in ruling the 'masses' with whips and swords; and in keeping the social mechanism functioning, without meaning or purpose: 'the individual hardly matters'. Clifford is not 'in touch' with anybody; his life is a negation of human contact. The wood in the park, which is to be the scene of Connie's regenerated existence and her rediscovery of human relationships, is to Clifford a piece of property, the sight of which makes him long for an heir. With a curiously impersonal desire he urges Connie to have a child. To Clifford sexual connections are merely transient sensations; what really matters in life is the outward form, the continuity of habitual associations—'the long, slow, habit of intimacy'. In the management of the mines Clifford finds an activity which compensates for his lack of human touch and flow: which fills him with a sense of mechanical power, power over men and things. And when Connie eventually leaves him for Mellors, Clifford lapses into the perverse, childlike relationship of maternal intimacy with his nurse, Mrs. Bolton. *Lady Chatterley's Lover*

CHATTERLEY, LADY (CONSTANCE): Née Reid: nowhere in Constance's life, in her marriage to the crippled and impotent baronet, or in her position as Lady of Wragby Hall, can she find any meaning or purpose, any satisfaction or fulfilment. Her isolation from people and the world around her, her lack of touch and contact, is for her a frightening loneliness. In a series of relationships—a love-affair before marriage, her relation to Clifford, an adulterous affair with Michaelis—she finds nothing of value, a vacuum of experience. Until she catches sight of Mellors the gamekeeper washing in his backyard: the sight of his nakedness is a 'visionary experience', 'the perfect, white, solitary nudity of a creature that lives alone'. In mutual sympathy, compassion, tenderness and desire they become lovers: and through the physical relationship with Mellors, she re-establishes living connection with the outside world, the world of living and growing things. Together in the wood, they discover the naked intimacy of touch and contact, and develop a new attitude to the world around them—an attitude of unrelenting hostility towards the industrialised world of coal and iron, which distorts true feeling and perverts natural relationship. Alone against the whole world, Connie and Mellors cherish and preserve the 'little flame' of their love; and in Connie's pregnancy they find a frail but powerful hope for the future. *Lady Chatterley's Lover*

CHATTERLEY, EMMA: Clifford's sister; she sometimes comes to Wragby, and her aristocratic, thin face triumphs at finding nothing altered—she would never forgive Connie for ousting her from her union in consciousness with her brother. *Lady Chatterley's Lover*

CHATTERLEY, SIR GEOFFREY: Father of Clifford, Emma and Herbert; a determined patriot, chopping down his trees and weeding men out of his colliery to shove them into the war; and himself being so safe and patriotic, he seems to Clifford 'intensely ridiculous'. He stands for England and Lloyd George as his forebears had stood for England and St. George —and he never knew there was a difference. Dies in 1918. *Lady Chatterley's Lover*

CHATTERLEY, HERBERT: Clifford's elder brother, killed in 1916, leaving Clifford heir to Wragby. *Lady Chatterley's Lover*

CICIO (FRANCESCO MARASCA): Southern-Italian member of the Natcha-Kee-Tawara travelling theatrical troupe; dark, rather tall and loose, with skin delicately tawny and slightly lustrous; a long, fine nose and a curling lip; with strange, fine black hair, close as fur, like an animal. Alvina Houghton notices especially his slender-brown hands, prehensile and dusky; his odd, graceful slouch, and his stupid, self-conscious, jeering smile. Physically he has a velvety, suave heaviness, fully and softly powerful. There is something mindless but *intent* about the forward reach of his head. On the day of

James Houghton's death, Cicio stands before Alvina and summons her, with a barely perceptible jerk of the head, to come with him; in his eyes there is a 'dark flicker of ascendency', and Alvina finds herself resolving into helpless submission. Alvina's relation to Cicio is always ambivalent: she responds deeply to his dark sensuality, and to his 'old beauty, formed through civilisation after civilisation'; but is repelled by his modern vulgarism and decadence, and his gold-digging materialism of an impoverished Italian. But ultimately she has no choice but to submit to the fate which sweeps her away with Cicio to Italy. *The Lost Girl*

CIPRIANO, DON: *see* Viedma, General (Don Cipriano)

COATES, MISS: Teacher in the dame's school at Cossethay which Anna Brangwen attends as a child. *The Rainbow*

COCHRANE, LADY: Acquaintance of Josephine Ford, who graciously gives her a box at the opera. *Aaron's Rod*

COLONEL, THE: Stout, rubicund and bald, a guest of Sir William Franks at Novara. *Aaron's Rod*

CONCHA: Daughter of Juana, Kate Leslie's housekeeper. About fourteen years old, a thick, heavy, barbaric girl, with a mass of black hair which she is always scratching. This 'belching savage' trespasses upon Kate's privacy with her malevolent mockery and jeering derision. *The Plumed Serpent*

CONNIE: A machinist at Thomas Jordan's Surgical Appliance Factory in Nottingham, where Paul Morel works as a clerk: with a mane of red hair and a face of apple blossom, and a murmuring voice, she is a lady despite her shabby frock. *Sons and Lovers*

CONSTABLE, ALGY: Dilettante friend of Francis and Angus, who flaps his eyelids like a crazy owl. *Aaron's Rod*

COOLEY, BENJAMIN (KANGAROO): Extraordinarily like a kangaroo, with a long, lean, pendulous face, and eyes set close together behind his pince-nez; and his body stout and firm. A man of forty or so, swarthy, with a small head and short-cropped hair; tall, but with a stoop and a drop of the head which diminishes his height. When he smiles, his face is sweet and charming, like a flower. Yet he is quite ugly. Kangaroo is leader of the Diggers, a para-military group which aims to seize political power in Australia by force, and impose order through a benevolent dictatorship, which Kangaroo would rule as a patriarch or a pope, representing 'the wise subtle spirit of life'. The state of Australia would be a kind of church, with 'the profound reverence for life and life's deepest urges as the motive power'. Kangaroo offers no creed or dogma, only his personal charisma—himself, in his 'heart of wisdom'. Richard Lovat Somers admires Kangaroo for his *absoluteness*, his 'strange, blind heroic obsession', and almost loves him for his *disinterestedness*, his pure, essential kindliness, a physically warm love that seems to make the corpuscles of the blood glow. But ultimately Somers rejects the love and the political allegiance: and then Kangaroo's love recoils back on itself, he becomes hideous, with his long, yellowish face and eyes close together, and a 'cold, dangerous, mindless hulk to his shoulders'; Lovat feels the intense hatred coming at him in cold waves, from the man now transformed into a 'Thing, a horror'. Kangaroo is shot during a riot created by the Diggers, and dies begging Somers to love him. Somers refuses: ' "I can't say it".' 'He didn't love Kangaroo.' *Kangaroo*

COPPARD, GEORGE: Father of Gertrude Morel, an engineer, a large, handsome, haughty man, proud of his fair skin and blue eyes, but more proud still of his integrity. *Sons and Lovers*

CRESSWELL, FREDDY: A friend of Leslie Tempest, broad-shouldered and pale-faced, with beautiful soft hair like red wheat, and laughing eyes and a whimsical, drawling manner of speech; a 'boy', irresponsible, lovable, a trifle pathetic. *The White Peacock*

CRICH, DIANA: Young daughter of Thomas Crich, who is tragically drowned in the lake at Shortlands during the water-party. *Women in Love*

CRICH, GERALD: Fair and sun-tanned, above middle height, almost exaggeratedly well-dressed; there is a strange, guarded look about him, as if he belongs to a creation different from that of the people around him. 'In his clear, northern flesh and fair hair is a glisten like sunshine refracted through crystals of ice'; 'so new, so unbroached, pure as an arctic thing'. But there is a significant, sinister stillness in his bearing, the lurking danger of his unsubdued temper. Beneath the gleaming, ice-cold beauty Birkin recognises the 'perfect good-humoured callousness, the strange glistening malice, glistening through the plausible ethics of productivity.' As a coal-mine owner, Gerald exercises power and control over men and things, fulfils himself by subjugating them to his will—he is the 'god of the machine', what he wants is 'the pure fulfilment of his own will in the struggle with natural conditions'. To Gerald what matters, in the mines and in society as a whole, is the great social productive machine; the sufferings and feelings of individuals hardly matter. What matters is the function, the pure instrumentality of the individual. The inhuman principle in this mechanical activity inspires Gerald with an almost religious exaltation: he finds his eternal and his infinite in 'the pure machine-principle of perfect co-ordination with one pure, complex, infinitely-repeated motion, like the spinning of a wheel'. In his individual life Gerald goes on living; but the meaning has collapsed out of him; and sometimes he feels the vacuum of his own unreality. After his father's death the emptiness is intolerable: he feels like a man hung in chains over the edge of an abyss, a bottomless void—if he falls, he will be gone for ever. He has to seek a reinforcement, his own single self will not sustain him. So he goes to Gudrun Brangwen, and finds in her an 'infinite relief': he pours into her all his 'pent-up darkness and corrosive death', and is whole again; while she subjects herself to the receiving of him, a vessel filled 'with his bitter potion of death'. Ultimately, when their relationship fails, the prospect of separation from Gudrun is intolerable for him: it demands that he stand by himself in sheer nothingness. Or he could kill her, and that would be a perfect, voluptuous pleasure. But Gerald is defeated: 'he was weak, but he did not want to rest, he wanted to go on and on, to the end; never again to stay, till he came to the end, that was all the desire that remained to him.' The end for Gerald is nothingness; what they find in the snow is 'mute, dead matter'—'the frozen carcase of a dead male'. *Women in Love*

CRICH, LAURA: Daughter of Thomas Crich, bride at the Crich wedding which opens *Women in Love*

CRICH, MRS. (CHRISTIANA): Wife of Thomas, a queer, unkempt figure, with a pale, yellowish face, and clear transparent skin, handsome, strongly marked features, and a tense, unseeing, predatory look. She seems like a woman with a monomania, furtive but heavily proud. Of a wild and overweening temper, she could never tolerate her husband's soft, half-appealing kindness to everyone, especially his employees. She rebels against his doctrine of charity, opposes him like a hawk—'with the fascinating beauty and abstraction of a hawk, she beat against the bars of his philanthrophy'. She is a prisoner, subject, recoiling from her husband's world of 'creeping democracy' into an isolation fierce and hard, an antagonism passive but terribly pure. She is consumed in a fierce tension of opposition, like the negative pole of a magnet; eccentric in behaviour, almost insane. *Women in Love*

CRICH, THOMAS: A tall, thin, careworn man with a thin, black beard; father of Laura, Gerald, Lottie, Basil, Diana and Winifred. A mine owner and employer of labour, he is a believer in charity and love of his neighbour. A single flame always burns in his heart, sustaining him through everything —the welfare of the people. So he is always excessively charitable and kind, to the detriment of his own business and his own being. In his heart he believes that he is united with his workmen in Christ, that essentially he is one of them, even their inferior; so the miners become his idol, and in them he worships 'the great, mindless, sympathetic godhead of humanity'. His relationship with his wife is deep and awful, a relation of utter inter-destruction. He becomes more and more hollow, his vitality bled from within him. All his life he has substituted pity and pretence for genuine relationship —and now in his last illness his pity is wearing thin, and a dread almost amounting to horror arises within him—the dread of recognising the truth. But before the armour of his pity really breaks, he dies, as an insect when its shell is cracked. *Women in Love*

CRICH, WINIFRED: A Crich daughter, an odd, sensitive, inflammable child, dark and quiet, detached, momentaneous. She has an instinctive critical faculty, and is a pure anarchist, a pure aristocrat at once. She accepts her equals and ignores with blind indifference her inferiors, existing quite singly and by herself, as if cut off from all purpose or continuity, existing simply moment by moment. *Women in Love*

CUMMINS, CHARLOTTE: Miss Cummins is a well-educated and sensitive woman engaged as a nurse and companion to the ageing Colin Urquhart. She has a passionate loyalty to his daughter, the Princess, and a curious affection, tinged with love, for the handsome, white-haired, courteous old man. After Colin's death, Miss Cummins becomes companion to the Princess, and they travel together. A certain distance is always maintained between them. Miss Cummins, intelligent and scholastic, has a passionate veneration for the Princess, who seems to her timeless, ageless, eternal; she feels for her a passionate tenderness, reverence, almost awe. Like the Princess, she is also virginal, with a look of puzzled surprise in her brown eyes; her skin pale and clear, her features well-modelled, but with a certain blankness of expression; and her voice hushed almost to a whisper. Miss Cummins accompanies the Princess and Domingo Romero on their ride into the Rocky Mountains; but her horse falls lame, and she has to return to the ranch, leaving the other two to go on alone. *The Princess*

CUNNINGHAM, JULIA: Née Bricknell; sister of Jim, a tall stag of a thing, hunched up like a witch—a real beauty. The wife of Robert Cunningham, she is contemplating living with Cyril Scott at his cottage in Dorset. *Aaron's Rod*

CUNNINGHAM, ROBERT: Married to Julia Bricknell; a fresh, stoutish young Englishman in khaki, a lieutenant about to be demobilised, when he would become a sculptor once more. His face has the blunt, voluptuous gravity of a young lion. *Aaron's Rod*

CURTISS, MRS.: Landlady of the cottage in the Isle of Wight where Siegmund MacNair and Helena Verden spend their holiday. A fragile little woman, of delicate, gentle manner. *The Trespasser*

CYPRIAN (CIPRIANITO): Son to Don Ramón Carrasco. Encouraged by his mother Doña Carlota, he is filled with high-principled disapproval of his father's activities in reviving the religion of Quetzalcoatl. *The Plumed Serpent*

D

DAKIN, MRS. L.: A tall, thin, shrew-faced woman; in the summer when coal production is slack, and the miners are sent home early, she stands on the hill-brow like a menace, watching them come up: 'What? Han' yer knocked off?' *Sons and Lovers*

DANIEL: Young boy, servant to Don Ramón. *The Plumed Serpent*

DANIELE: Assistant of Giovanni, Lady Chatterley's gondolier; beautiful, tall, and well-shapen, with a good-looking man's face, a little like a lion. He is a 'real man', like Mellors, dignified and unprostituted. *Lady Chatterley's Lover*

D'ARCY, AGNES: An erect, intelligent girl with magnificent auburn hair; a friend of Leslie Tempest. *The White Peacock*

DARRINGTON, MINETTE: A girl with bobbed, blonde hair cut in the artist fashion; small and delicately made, with fair colouring and large, innocent blue eyes. An acquaintance of Rupert Birkin and mistress of Julius Halliday, she is attracted to Gerald Crich, who admires the delicate floweriness in her form and at the same time, her attractive 'grossness of spirit'. She has beautiful eyes, flower-like and naked, on which there seems to float an iridescence, 'a sort of film of disintegration, like oil on water'. She is compelled to Gerald, slave-like; she has to discover the secret of his male being, and become a victim in his power. She greets his approach with the look of a violated slave, whose fulfilment lies in her further and further violation. *Women in Love*

DAWES, BAXTER: A blacksmith, husband of Clara, the woman who becomes Paul Morel's mistress; a big, well-set man, handsome with his white skin, with a clear golden tinge, and his soft brown hair; but his eyes, protruding, dark-brown and quick-shifting, are dissolute, and his mouth sensual. His whole manner expresses a cowed defiance, and his speech is dirty, with a kind of rottenness. Married to Clara, he never succeeded in awakening the woman in her—she remained only half-alive, dormant, deadened. When Clara becomes Paul's lover, there is between him and Baxter a confirmed enmity, and yet a peculiar feeling of intimacy. Baxter lies in wait for Paul and beats him up, but suffers himself a kind of spiritual sickness, a dissolution of soul. After his illness, Clara returns to him, penitent and self-sacrificial. *Sons and Lovers*

DAWES, CLARA: A blonde with a sullen expression and a defiant air, with scornful grey eyes, and a skin like white honey; a full mouth, with a slightly lifted upper lip, that 'did not know whether it was raised in scorn of all men, or out of eagerness to be kissed'. But Clara believes the former: separated from a frustrating, unfulfilled marriage, she becomes a passionate devotee of Women's Rights, and a confirmed man-hater. But in her love-affair with Paul Morel, she experiences transcendent ecstasies of passion—'the naked hunger and inevitability of his loving her, something strong and blind and ruthless in its primitiveness, made the hour almost terrible to her.' But she wants a relationship more permanent than Paul can offer: she craves for surety, stability; in her love for Paul she discovers herself, and can stand distinct and complete, having 'received her confirmation'; but she never believes that her life belongs to him. There is no stability in Paul: at least her husband has a kind of 'manly dignity', whereas Morel is evanescent, not sure ground for a woman to stand on. She visits Baxter in hospital, wanting to make restitution; he can offer her a relationship of permanence and stability, if it is only a permanence and stability of self-sacrifice. *Sons and Lovers*

DEKKER, FRANZ (FRANCIS): Tall, handsome and well-coloured, graceful in everything, in his elegant figure, in the pose of his handsome head, in the modulation of his voice. A dilettante, companion of Angus, 'working' in Rome, he briefly patronises Aaron Sisson in Florence. *Aaron's Rod*

DEL TORRE, THE MARCHESA: An American woman from the Southern States, she has lived most of her life in Europe; the wife of the Marchese. She is about forty years old, very handsome, full-bosomed, sad and remote; she seems to Aaron like a modern Cleopatra, brooding for an Anthony. She is attracted to Aaron, and his flute-playing gives her a glimpse of freedom from 'the dungeon of feelings and moral necessities'

35

which is her life. He is fascinated by her 'terribly modern elegance', carefully made up, with a touch of exaggeration that frightens him; he thinks her wonderful and sinister, she affects him almost with a touch of horror. As a lover she uses him to gratify her 'pure, unalloyed desire', but ignores the individual man that he is with an indifference that startles him. Ultimately she has no power over him: 'his soul stood apart and decided'. *Aaron's Rod*

DEL TORRE, THE MARCHESE (MANFREDI): A little, intense Italian in Colonel's uniform; with blue eyes, hair cut very short, and a head that looks hard and rather military; he resembles a gnome. He fears the female will, and strongly objects to woman as the initiator of desire. Aaron Sisson listens respectfully to his confidences, and then seduces his wife the Marchesa. *Aaron's Rod*

DENYS, LOUIE: A tall, graceful girl of the drooping type, elaborately gowned in heliotrope linen; a friend of Leslie Tempest. *The White Peacock*

DI LANTI, SIGNOR: An old, old Italian elegant in side-curls, who peels off his gloves and studies his formalities with a delightful mid-Victorian dash. *Aaron's Rod*

DIONYS, COUNT: *see* Psanek, Count Johann Dionys

DUG: A grinning Australian workman, who places Richard Lovat Somers on sight as either a 'Bolshy' or a 'Fritz'. *Kangaroo*

DUKES, TOMMY: A Brigadier-General, guest and friend of Clifford Chatterley; lean, freckled and Irish-looking. He believes that the 'life of the Mind' is rooted in spite and envy; and that real knowledge should come out of the whole corpus of the consciousness, out of the belly and penis as much as the brain and mind. He believes in having 'a good heart, a chirpy penis, a lively intelligence, and the courage to say "shit" in front of a lady.' Nevertheless, as a confirmed 'mental-lifer,' Dukes has none of these accomplishments. He speaks, like Mellors, of the possibility of regenerated relations between man and man, and man and woman, in the future, of the possibility of a 'democracy of touch'; but he remains in actuality a self-confessed 'cerebrating machine'. *Lady Chatterley's Lover*

DURANT, ALFRED: The youngest son of Mr. and Mrs. Durant; a collier who enlists in the Navy at the age of twenty. He is missed by his mother who had spoiled and pampered him; and also by Louisa Lindley, who recalls him as a laughing, warm lad with something kindly and rich about him. The days will be colder with his absence. But her father the Reverend Ernest Lindley feels that the wholesome naval discipline, and the standards of duty and honour, will be just the thing to save Alfred from the ubiquitous dangers of intemperance. On his return from the service he is a tall, handsome, slender and sunburnt man, with hazel eyes. The sight of him absorbed in tender grief for his dying father, and offering careful solicitude to his suffering mother, makes Louisa feel again the great attraction of his natural spontaneous, emotional nature. But after his father's death, he remains separate from her, puts himself in the position of a social inferior and avoids personal connection. He has a strong, shrinking sensitivity before women, almost a chastity, which makes him feel uneasy, inadequate, despicable, for all his physical health and fitness, and all his manly pursuits. So he is miserable beneath his healthy cheerfulness, envying in others the ability to satisfy instinct directly and unconsciously—even the stupid and brutal. With the death of his mother, Alfred loses the centre of his life; but in Louisa, who looks after his mother in her illness, he sees an ideal, of everything that is beyond him, of revelation and exquisiteness; though she seems distant, remote, inaccessible, yet she is something steady and immovable and eternal. He realises that he loves her and must marry her. In the eyes of the vicar and his family the marriage of their daughter to the young collier seems imprudent, and socially unthinkable—it represents a dreadful blot on their shabby-genteel escutcheon of respectability. But in the face of attempts to scorn and belittle him by the superior members of the vicarage, Alfred clings to his independence and self-respect. He will have what his life demands: Louisa. *The Daughters of the Vicar*

DURANT, MRS.: Mother of Alfred Durant; a woman who would have liked to be easy in her life, but who had the misfortune to have a rough and turbulent family, and a slothful husband. So her good-looking square face is peevish, with the air of having been compelled all her life into unwilling service, and unwilling exercise of control. Managing her riotous and hard-drinking sons had been an unwelcome fret; but she loves the youngest boy, Alfred, and is angry and resentful when he enlists in the Navy. She would have liked him to be a gentleman, but he was too eager to join other men, in the pit or in the service. And yet at bottom Alfred does not satisfy her, because he does not seem manly enough: his tastes for reading and music inspire in her a grudging tenderness, even pity, but never respect. She wants Alfred to be self-sufficient, and to go his own way without a woman; but he is too dependent on her. She makes him into her baby, loves him for it, and is then perversely contemptuous of him. When she dies he is left helpless, empty, centreless, but setting gradually and definitely towards another woman, Louisa Lindley. *The Daughters of the Vicar*

DURANT, WALTER: A big elderly man, with a great grey beard, who grunts in a deep muttering voice, and stares vacantly into the fire. Husband of Mrs. Durant, father of Alfred. He is a very large man with slow, sluggish movements, taciturn and inert, silent and dull. His slothful existence seems to develop naturally into a fatal paralysis where he lies in monolithic inertness, without understanding or recognition, until his lifeless bulk sinks into the monumental paralysis of death. *The Daughters of the Vicar*

E

EASTWOOD, MAJOR: An acquaintance of Yvette Saywell, he is the sort of man one immediately associates with winter sports, skating and skiing. He has a magnificent figure, an athletic, prominent chest, abstract blue eyes, and smooth, naked cheeks. He has resigned his commission to live with Mrs. Fawcett, who awaits her divorce; and their friendship towards Yvette is regarded as morally infamous by the Reverend Arthur Saywell. Yet essentially their morality is higher than his—the

Major feels 'a curious indignation against life, because of its false morality'. His tenderness for Mrs. Fawcett is based on 'a sense of outraged justice'. *The Virgin and the Gipsy*

EDWARDS, FREDERICK (FRED): An acquaintance of the Carringtons, a blond Englishman with a little brush moustache and strange blue eyes, which always try to look sentimental. His brilliant career of fox-hunting, gallant behaviour and outrageous flirting is somewhat marred by a kick in the face from St. Mawr, and a consequent facial disfigurement. *St. Mawr*

ELLIS, ELLIE: 'Floss-haired baby' of the Ellis family at Wandoo. *The Boy in the Bush*

ELLIS, GRACE: Twin daughter of Jacob Ellis, sister of Monica; she has the same thin, soft, slightly tanned, warm-looking face, a little wild. She has big eyes, a big nose and a gentle heart. There is an appealing, sad wisdom at the bottom of her. *The Boy in the Bush*

ELLIS, GRAN: A delicate old lady, with a lace cap, white curly hair, and an ivory face. She is the 'presiding deity' of the Ellis family, though mostly invisible; there is something weird in her remoteness. She gives Jack Grant some strange pieces of advice, which he nevertheless remembers: urging him to 'trust the glow of his spirit', because that is God—'yourself is God'. *The Boy in the Bush*

ELLIS, HARRY: Six-year-old son of Jacob Ellis, fat, blue-eyed and handsome, strong as a baby bull. *The Boy in the Bush*

ELLIS, JACOB: Self-effacing father of the Ellis family, who dies at the same time as the Grandmother. *The Boy in the Bush*

ELLIS, JANE: Monica's illegitimate daughter by Easu. A defiant little girl hated by her mother. *The Boy in the Bush*

ELLIS, KATIE: One of the younger Ellis children; younger than Lennie but pretty near his size. *The Boy in the Bush*

ELLIS, LENNIE: Son of Jacob, a boy with a beautiful little face, with an odd pathos like some lovely girl, grey eyes that could change to black; winsome and whimsical, 'a funny kid', given to singing and quoting scraps of Latin and poetry. There are three things he does exceptionally well—riding, laughing and boasting. Refuses the opportunity of an English education, and after getting a girl into trouble, marries at seventeen. *The Boy in the Bush*

ELLIS, MA: A brown-haired woman with a tired look, wife of Jacob; drawn and distant, she is a drudge who takes no notice of anybody. *The Boy in the Bush*

ELLIS, THE MISSES: Three maiden aunts of the Ellis family who hang around the bedside of the dying Gran, audibly weeping. Her only bequest to them is her hope that virginity will be its own reward. *The Boy in the Bush*

ELLIS, MONICA: Twin daughter of Jacob Ellis, with her darkish fair hair, queer yellow-grey eyes, shy and wild, but with the effrontery of a wildcat under a bush. She slinks like a lean young panther. Monica assumes from the outset a 'proprietorial' interest in Jack, extending to him an impulsive affectionateness, a winsome tenderness, and a fierce appeal. She loves in Jack his 'delicate, English, virgin quality', his shyness and natural purity. But she is disgruntled by Jack's reticent hanging-back, his lack of decision; she keeps herself mute and closed, like a shut-up bud—withdraws into a luminous distance, remote. Later, pregnant with Red Easu's child, she lives with Pink-eye Percy, but when Jack returns she submits to *him*—he remains to her 'the eternal stranger'; he will never belong to her, she must belong to him. He is a doom, a fate she can no longer withstand. *The Boy in the Bush*

ELLIS, OG and MAGOG: The twin Ellis boys, 'called for giants 'cos they're so small'. *The Boy in the Bush*

ELLIS, RED EASU: A big, loose-jointed, domineering man, swivel-eyed, with a slow, laconic assurance, and a sense of great power. The head of the Red Ellis clan, he has a certain handsomeness, but Jack Grant detects in his meaningful, evil smile, a malevolent principle, a kind of venom. Easu assumes towards Jack the instinctive hostility of the colonial towards the old mastery of the old country, brutal and retrogressive. When Easu makes advances to Monica Ellis, the enmity crystallises, and Jack feels an ecstasy of hate, keener than love, an orgasm of deadly gratification. On Jack's return from the North, Easu is married, and changed for the worse: bawling and bullying, humiliated and ugly. His wife Sarah Anne is common, but with a vulgar *suffisance*; resplendent and gorgeous on Sundays, she spends the whole week in preparation, wreathed in immense iron curling pins. Easu has gone heavier, stuck and inert, the life gone out of him. When the struggle between him and Jack reaches a crisis, Jack is forced to kill him in self-defence. And yet the killing is merely the enactment of Jack's inevitable, god-given fate: 'Inside himself was the reality and the assurance. Easu was dead. It was a good thing.' *The Boy in the Bush*

ELLIS, RED HERBERT: A boy of nineteen, uncouth and savagely shy; injured in an accident, he is skilfully nursed by Jack Grant, and ineffectively held down by his brothers, Alan and Ross; the convulsive struggles of the sick man are stilled by the quiet, impersonal patience of Jack. *The Boy in the Bush*

ELLIS, TOM: Son of Jacob by his first marriage, becomes paternal head of the family when his father dies. He becomes a close friend of Jack Grant, and accompanies him on his journey into the bush. *The Boy in the Bush*

EMMA: A machinist at Thomas Jordan's Surgical Appliance Factory in Nottingham, where Paul Morel works as a clerk; she is 'rather plain, rather old, and condescending'. *Sons and Lovers*

ETHEL: Friend and *confidante* of Ursula Brangwen. *The Rainbow*

EVANS, MR.: A red-moustached Welshman with a slightly injured look in his pale blue eyes. He has settled in Australia and describes to Harriet Somers the tough process of reconciling oneself to Australian life. *Kangaroo*

EZEQUIEL: Younger son of Juana, Kate Leslie's housekeeper. A wild, shy youth, very erect and proud, half-savage—a gentleman in his barbarism. He offers to protect Kate's room at night, reassuring her with his pistol, his manly courage, and his fierce, resonant snoring. A proud worker in the fields,

Ezequiel becomes an enthusiastic 'man of Quetzalcoatl'. *The Plumed Serpent*

F

FANNY: A shy little blonde maid of the Carringtons, who is terrified by the subtle and insidious creepings of the Indian, Phoenix. *St. Mawr*

FANNY: A machinist at Thomas Jordan's Surgical Appliance Factory in Nottingham, where Paul Morel works as a clerk; a hunchback, with a long, rather heavy face and bright brown hair. She is morbidly sensitive about her deformity, but kind to Paul, who admires her beautiful hair. *Sons and Lovers*

FAWCETT, MRS.: A small woman, thin as a child, with a rather large nose, and with 'the wide, resentful eyes of a spoilt Jewess'. She is the wife of a well-known and wealthy engineer, and awaiting her divorce she lives with Major Eastwood. Her friendship for Yvette Saywell earns the contempt of the Reverend Arthur; but Mrs. Fawcett is in fact herself highly moral: she feels a burning moral indignation against her husband, who ill-treated her; 'she was intensely moral, so moral that she was a divorcée'. *The Virgin and the Gipsy*

FELIPA: Sixteen-year-old cousin and associate louse-hunter of Concha and Maria. *The Plumed Serpent*

FFRENCH, MR.: An elderly *littérateur*, more proud of his social standing (which is not very high) than his literature; an English snob of the old order, living abroad. *Aaron's Rod*

FIELD: The Chatterleys' manservant. *Lady Chatterley's Lover*

FIELD, JOHN: Son of a well-to-do tradesman, and the teenage Gertrude Morel's 'young man'. He suffers from a conflict between his thwarted ambitions towards 'the ministry', and his father's determination to put him 'into the business'. He later finds some consolation in marrying his landlady, a forty-year-old widow of property; but Mrs. Morel continues to cherish his memory and his Bible. *Sons and Lovers*

FLINT, MRS.: A farmer's wife, tenant of the Chatterleys'; the mother of a perky little red-haired baby, Josephine, which arouses maternal yearnings in Connie. *Lady Chatterley's Lover*

FORBES, DUNCAN: An artist, friend of Constance Chatterley and her sister Hilda; a quiet, almost taciturn young man, who accompanies them in Venice. Formerly in love with Connie, he volunteers to pose as the father of Mellors' child. *Lady Chatterley's Lover*

FORBES, MRS.: The lover of Alfred Brangwen (Junior); a tall woman with white hair, full of dignity, straight, rather hard, a curious, separate creature. Superior and educated, she impresses Alfred's brother Tom, and makes him conscious of the limitations of his own life; but he feels there is something 'chilling' about her. Ultimately she seems to him something cold, something alien, 'as if she were not a woman, but a human being using up human life for cold, unliving purposes.' *The Rainbow*

FORD, JOSEPHINE: (Incorrectly introduced as Josephine Hay.) Jim Bricknell's fiancée. An artist, a cameo-like girl, with black hair done neatly and tight in the French mode; with brilliant colouring, and strangely drawn eyebrows. Her movements are very quiet and well-bred, perhaps too quiet: they have the 'dangerous impassivity' of the Bohemian. After a number of unsuccessful attempts, she succeeds in seducing Aaron, taking him as an antidote to her own spiritual loneliness. *Aaron's Rod*

FRAMLEY, BOB: Friend of the Saywell girls, with his sisters Ella and Lottie. *The Virgin and the Gipsy*

FRANCIS: *see* Dekker, Franz

FRANKS, LADY: Wife of Sir William Franks: short, rather plump, but erect and definite, with a self-righteous assurance based on her wealth, and her position as hostess dispensing charity. She reminds Aaron of Queen Victoria. *Aaron's Rod*

FRANKS, SIR WILLIAM: A very wealthy self-made man with a villa at Novara, who entertains Aaron Sisson: a small, clean old man with a thin white beard, and white hair like spun glass, courteous and benevolent, a little affected, but pleasant. Frail, old and afraid of death, he wants to be young, to live; but in the absence of spontaneous vitality he demands—and gets—the homage due to his wealth and property. *Aaron's Rod*

FRANKSTONE, DR.: Female doctor of Physics in Nottingham University College: a materialist who argues that life consists in a complexity of physical and chemical activities, without any special meaning or purpose. But to Ursula life seems to be more than mechanical energy—it is a consummation, a being infinite; to be oneself is not to be an accidental conjunction of impersonal forces, but to be a supreme, gleaming triumph of infinity. *The Rainbow*

FROST, MISS: A handsome, vigorous woman, with grey-white hair and gold-rimmed spectacles; strong and generous, she is a musician by nature, an itinerant teacher of music by profession. During the first twenty-five years of Alvina Houghton's life, Miss Frost the governess is her greatest personal friend and companion. Miss Frost rather despises James Houghton, considering him a hypocrite, and detesting his fairy fantasy. The whole morale of Manchester House thus devolves on Miss Frost: she sees her primary obligation and responsibility as being the ruling of the house with a firm, quiet hand, and the protection of Alvina and Mrs. Houghton. For twenty-five years, the strong, protective governess rears and tends her lamb; and does not live to see Alvina rebel entirely against the high-minded purity of her governess's teaching. *The Lost Girl*

G

GALL, ALICE: A short, plump girl, with daring, rebellious eyes, a friend of the Beardsalls' and Saxtons'. Mocking and ironical, she is 'wild and lawless' on the surface, but upright and amenable at heart. She marries a pillar of the Church, Percival Charles, who lives in an eternal Sunday suit, and wallows in Bibles when he goes to bed. *The White Peacock*

GARCIA: A young Mexican, a professor in the university; a short, soft young fellow of twenty-seven or eight who 'wrote the inevitable poetry of sentiment, had been in the government, and was longing to go to New York'. A socialist intellectual, and a passionate defender of revolutionary art. *The Plumed Serpent*

GEOFFREY: A broad-shouldered, watchful, taciturn young man from Alpine France, a member of the Natcha-Kee-Tawara travelling theatrical troupe; the intimate friend and companion of Cicio. *The Lost Girl*

GEORGE, MR: A lawyer who looks after Jack Grant on his arrival in Australia: a stout, breezy, rumbustical old gentleman, with a tongue like a razor; in Jack's eyes stout and decidedly old-fashioned, a shabby, provincial-looking man, rather than the 'hearty colonial hero' of his mother's reminiscences. He plies Jack with effusively abundant advice on colonial *mores*; and is shocked by Jack's lack of motivation to become a 'gentleman'. *The Boy in the Bush*

GIOVANNI: Gondolier hired by Connie Chatterley and her sister in Venice; a childish, impetuous fellow, who hopes to be able to prostitute himself to the English ladies. *Lady Chatterley's Lover*

GIOVANNI: Cicio's uncle. A smallish, brigandish-looking fellow, with his cloak over his nose and his hat over his eyes; according to his brother Pancrazio he is 'not quite sensible'. *The Lost Girl*

GONZALEZ: Don Cipriano's chauffeur. *The Plumed Serpent*

GRAHAM, ALEXANDER: An Australian, taking a medical degree in Edinburgh, practising with the Woodhouse Doctor. A man of medium height, dark colouring and dark eyes, and a body which seems to move inside his clothing. Alvina Houghton finds him attractive—fascinating, but slightly repulsive—and they become engaged. She is divided between a rational perception of the man's insignificance, and a sensual appreciation of his darker potencies. When he goes to Australia, the sensual appeal dies away, and Alvina returns to her former demureness. She will not follow him. *The Lost Girl*

45

GRANDMOTHER, MEG'S: A hard-visaged, bosomless dame clad in thick, black, cloth-like armour, sighing into her whisky. She has been a big woman, but now her shapeless, broken figure looks pitiful. Even bedridden, she clings to life like a louse to a pig's back. *The White Peacock*

GRANT, GENERAL: A military gentleman in colonial service, officer in Her Majesty's Army; husband of Katie, father of Jack. The General is handsome, pleasant, always genteelly dressed, and indisputably 'good'; but to his son Jack always 'unreal and fantastic'. *The Boy in the Bush*

GRANT, JACK: 'The boy in the bush'; he arrives in Australia looking like a lamb; good-looking, with dark blue eyes and the complexion of a girl—perhaps a little too lamb-like to be convincing. His parents have exiled him from England because of his fondness for 'low company', and his indifference to the higher claims of society. Jack is always homesick 'for some place which he had never known'—and he always silently but deeply hates wherever he is. But he grows to love the Ellis family with a steady, rooted passion. Jack feels that his life is governed by a kind of fate or doom: he has no free choice about his actions. He himself is an isolated, separate living thing; and somewhere outside him is a terrible dark god who decrees his fate. He feels a powerful love for Monica Ellis, together with a corresponding desire to preserve himself from her, to remain free and alone, in the sanctity of his own isolation. He wants to marry Monica; but misunderstanding her actions, the 'deep, burning life-anger' in him hardens into black, rocky indifference, and he leaves with Tom Ellis for the North. He disappears into the silent timelessness and motionless aloofness of the bush, where the gods of the old world, his father's world, have crumbled to dust. But in the bush, the land untouched by man, he still craves for some object for his passion to settle on, and discovers that freedom is unattainable as long as a man desires; the only freedom lies in the fulfilment of desire. So on his return Jack seeks to fulfil the several desires of his soul, each sanctioned by the utterance of the 'dark god': he kills Easu, marries Monica and subordinates her to his will, and attempts to incorporate Mary Rath into his life as a second wife; but she is not having any. We leave Jack confidently drawing into the orbit of his desires the young daughter of Boyd Blessington. *The Boy in the Bush*

GRANT, JOHN: Eccentric old cousin of Jack Grant, a thin man in a red flannel nightcap who sits in bed under a green umbrella. On his death he bequeaths a substantial farm to Jack. *The Boy in the Bush*

GRANT, KATIE: Australian-born mother of Jack, she is a warm, flushed, rather muddled woman, kindly in an off-hand humorous way, warm with a jolly sensuousness, and 'good in a wicked sort of way'. She follows her husband, whom she loves, 'laughing sensuously' across seven seas, quarrelling with nobody, at home wherever she goes, in true colonial fashion. There is about her a sense of great, unfenced spaces, that puts the ordinary ladies rather at a loss. 'A real colonial, from the newest, wildest, remotest colony.' *The Boy in the Bush*

GRENFEL, HENRY: A young soldier who appears suddenly and unexpectedly on the farm occupied by Banford and March: with a ruddy, roundish, face, rather long, fairish hair; blue, very bright and sharp eyes; his skin seems to glisten. He examines the girls with a sharp, impersonal curiosity under-lying his look of baffled wonder. To March, he is the fox: she cannot see him otherwise. He watches her in curiosity and fascination: her slim, well-shaped legs, her knot of dark hair. He is amused by the girls, by their scornful, cynical attitude to the farming life they have chosen. 'There wants a man about the place!' he says. He persuades the girls to let him stay on the farm, helps readily with the work, but likes best to be alone, half-hidden, watching; free to exercise his insatiable, sharp-eyed, impersonal curiosity. He particularly likes March, is piqued by her, and her dark eyes make an elate excitement rise within him. Then shrewdly, calculating, it occurs to him to marry her and take over the farm. He cares nothing that she is older: he feels himself master of her. Sly and subtle as he is, he knows that March will not submit to a direct attack or proposition: she must be stalked, furtively and secretly, circumvented by superior cunning and the mesmeric power of the hunter. He is truly a hunter, and wants

47

to bring March down as his quarry, to make her his wife. So he approaches her, soft and subtle as a cat, and imperceptibly, without startling her, draws her into his power. In a startled moment of consciousness March confesses to Henry her fascination with the fox: and her identification of the animal with himself; and as Banford's cross, fretful voice calls from upstairs, summoning March to bed, the soldier forces her with his soft, insidious power to agree to marriage. That night Henry overhears Banford and March in their room, Banford plaintively expressing her jealousy and anxiety, March comforting her in her soft, deep, tender voice. Immediately he goes out with the gun, looking for something: and as the fox prowls stealthily around the chicken coop, Henry shoots him. As the antagonism between him and Banford grows, he curses her under his breath, threatening to pay her back: 'You're a nasty little thing, you are!' And he is filled with rage as he sees the frail little Banford struggling across the fields with parcels, and March striding hurriedly down from the farm in manly anxiety and desire to help her friend. When, with a shock of surprise, Henry sees March for the first time in a dress, he is overwhelmed by appreciation of her soft, womanly body moving in her clothes; she is soft and accessible, and the thought goes home to him like an 'everlasting responsibility'; he feels more a man, quiet and grave, with something of the heaviness of male destiny upon him. March agrees to marry him; but when he returns to his camp, she returns to Banford, and writes telling him she's changed her mind. Henry is livid with rage and fury at this obstacle to the enactment of his destiny: to have March. His fury concentrates on the one irritating thorn in his flesh, Banford. Apparently by accident, but with a deeper, more inexorable fate underlying it, a tree felled by Henry kills Banford. The inner necessity of his life fulfils itself: he has won, and he is glad. *The Fox*

GREY: Garrulous coachman, who has been driving from Fremantle to Albany 'week in, week out, years without end, amen.' A man with a thin red face, a black beard, and queer grey eyes with a mocking sort of secret; formerly a servant, he eloped to Australia with his employer, Miss Ethel. *The Boy in the Bush*

GREY, MISS: Headmistress of the Grammar School which Ursula Brangwen attends; she has a certain silvery, schoolmistressy beauty of character. *The Rainbow*

GUEST, ANGUS: A dilettante, companion of Francis Dekker, 'working' in Rome; with a pale, thin face, a rimless monocle, and wide light blue eyes. He and Francis briefly patronise Aaron Sisson in Florence. *Aaron's Rod*

GUILLERMO: A *peon* with a grudge against Don Ramón Carrasco, who leads an assassination attempt, encouraged by the promise of a reward from the Knights of Cortés. Injured in the attack, he is subsequently executed/sacrificed/murdered by Cipriano on the 'night of Huitzilopochtli'. *The Plumed Serpent*

H

HALLIDAY, JULIUS: A swarthy, slender young man, with long, solid black hair, and a naive, warm vapid smile. His eyes are hazel-yellow, warm and confused, broken in their expression. His face is weak, slightly disintegrate, but with a moving beauty of its own. He combines a religious mania with a fascination for obscenity: he wants a pure lily with a Botticelli face on the one hand, and on the other hand he must have Minette, the harlot, to defile himself with. Birkin thinks he is 'really insane'. *Women in Love*

HAMMOND, ARNOLD B.: A writer, friend and guest of Sir Clifford Chatterley. A tall, thin fellow, with a wife and two children, 'but much more closely connected with a typewriter'; a believer in 'the life of the mind', he equates sexual emotions with excretory functions. *Lady Chatterley's Lover*

HAMPSON: A fair, slender man of some thirty-five years; a former acquaintance of Siegmund MacNair, they meet again on the Isle of Wight. A believer in intensity in life, in vivid soul-experience and physical excitement, the prospect of a return to reality seems to him like the embrace of a leper. *The Trespasser*

HANNELE (COUNTESS JOHANNA ZU RASSENTLOW): A fair woman with soft, delicate, dark blonde hair, full of strands of gold and tarnished gold and shadow; with a beautiful, fine skin, and a fresh and luminous face, with a certain quick gleam of life about it. She is a refugee in defeated Germany; forced to work for her living, she has a studio with her friend Mitchka, where she makes and sells little dolls, and is quite successful. Her masterpiece is the model of her lover Captain Hepburn, a British officer. Although she can make a doll of him, and even mischievously and daringly display it in her shop-window, still her heart always melts in her when he looks straight at her with his black eyes, and his curious, bright, unseeing look that is more like second sight than direct human vision. She never knows what he sees when he looks at her. Yet she is bitter about their love-affair: he is so ineffectual, so indecisive, so indifferent to the claims of everyday life. But she can't help being in love with him: with his hands, his strange, fascinating physique, his incalcuable presence; she loves the way he puts his feet down, the way he moves his legs as he walks, the mould of his loins, the way he drops his head, the strange, dark, unthinking vacancy of his brow. But he never *says* anything: words stray out of him in the need to make conversation, but essentially he never speaks. She battles with herself. When he caresses her, with the magic of an almost indefinable caress, she wants to stiffen herself in resistance, to draw away and have nothing to do with him, while he is so half-hearted and unsatisfactory. But his soft, straying voice spins gossamer threads around her, so she cannot struggle; she lets him kiss her, though her heart groans in rebellion. When the Captain is absent, Hannele almost forgets him, finding it difficult to remember what he is like—he disappears out of her, losing his significance. She cannot understand the nature of his influence, why she should become entangled with someone so insignificant, so unreal. She has seriously compromised herself—a German associating with a married English officer—for a man who seems little more than a mere puppet. But still she has a lurking suspicion that there might be something else: and so she awaits him. Then instantly she hears the slow, straying purr of his voice, she knows there is something else—she feels immediately the reality of his presence, and the corresponding unreality of her own German men-friends. Yet when his wife arrives to claim him, he goes to her unquestioningly; his own personal needs, desires, wishes—if he has any—don't seem to count. Hannele feels he is hardly normal, hardly human. When Mrs. Hepburn confides in Hannele her suspicions about Mitchka, and details episodes from their life together; when Hannele sees the married couple together—the little woman playing her fantasy romance, the Captain submissive and effaced, tame and obedient—she is appalled by the relationship. She cannot tolerate his acquiescent meekness, the way he does what she tells him, going off when she sends him away, like a servant, performing all his pledges and promises. She reflects on her own attraction to the Captain, trying to conceive what it is that holds her. She realises that the secret of his magnetism is *charm*: but when that charm isn't working, he seems to her stupid, an ass, a vulgar, limited person; an inferior, slightly pretentious individual. She hopes he will stay away from her. But still the charm goes on working, even in his absence: as she imagines the strange look, like destiny, in his wide-open, staring black eyes; the beautiful lines of his brow, that always seemed to have a cloud on it; the slow elegance of his straight, beautiful legs as he walked, the exquisiteness of his dark, slender chest—the snake of desire bites her heart. Then when she thinks of him in relation to his wife, belittled and humiliated, the charm disappears. But ultimately, though she suspects that his charm is really an illusion, perhaps it is an illusion more real and significant than other people's disillusion. She prefers to be under the spell of his charm, rather than faced with the distaste and vulgarity of disillusion. Perhaps the long disillusion of life, like the Captain's marriage, is falser than illusion. Life is all a choice; and she chooses the glamour, the magic, the charm, the illusion, the spell: she refuses to give up the Captain's doll to Mrs. Hepburn. Alexander goes away after his wife's death, and Hannele becomes engaged to the Herr Regierungsrat von Poldi; she would like to marry him. He makes her feel like a queen in exile: no one has ever kissed her hand as he kisses it, with a sudden stillness and a strange, chivalric abandon of himself. But when Alexander turns up, she hears his voice like a noise that sounds in the night; the world seems to split under her eyes, and show the darkness inside. Together they climb the glacier, and in their mutual hostility Alexander reviles the mountains—he refuses to share the exaltation, the uplift, the braced-up jollity of the surrounding trippers; he cannot participate in their feelings. Hannele is puzzled, touched with amazement, wonder, and fascination—to what country does he belong? To what dark, different atmosphere? She concludes that he wants her to love him; that he is offended because she sold his doll in Munich, and this explanation flatters her vanity—she feels quite glowing and triumphant. But he is filled with a passionate silence and imperiousness, a curious, dark, masterful force supplanting thought in him. She feels he is forcing her, bullying her into loving him; that he wants in his silent, black, overbearing soul to compel her, to have power over her. She is confident she will not be bullied. She probably loves him; but she wants him to go down on his knees; she will not have a dark-eyed, bullying little master. He is a puzzle to her: eternally incomprehensible. There seems to be no logic in his feelings or his sayings: which makes her uneasy, but is also fascinating. And yet still she will not give in to his black passion—she will demand love on equal terms. Will she submit? For he, in his incomprehensible darkness, will never submit. *The Captain's Doll*

HARBY, MR.: Headmaster of Brinsley Street school, short, thick-set, and rather common, but good-looking, with shapely brows and nose, and a great hanging moustache. He is bullying and threatening, universally hated for his authoritarianism. The one motive in his life is to exercise blind, despotic authority over the school. To Ursula the situation seems contradictory: Mr. Harby is so strong, such a man, with strength and male power, and a certain blind, native beauty. She might have liked him as a man, and here he stands bullying over such a trifle as a boy's speaking out without permission. He was imprisoned in a task too small and petty for him, yet which he fulfils in servile acquiescence, to earn a living. *The Rainbow*

HARBY, MISS VIOLET: Daughter of Mr. Harby and a teacher at Brinsley Street school; rather like her father, jolty, jerky and bossy. *The Rainbow*

HARDY, MRS.: The Squire's lady at Shelly Hall; in her the

Brangwen women see 'the further life' of knowledge and 'extended being'; in her they live imaginatively 'the life beyond'. *The Rainbow*

HASAN: Julius Halliday's Oriental manservant: he looks elegant, almost aristocratic, but is half a savage. His face is immutable, aristocratic-looking, tinged slightly with grey under the skin. Looking at him, Birkin feels a slight sickness, feeling the slight greyness as an ash or corruption, seeing in the aristocratic inscrutability of expression a nauseating, bestial stupidity. *Women in Love*

HEADLEY, DR.: A doctor at the maternity hospital in Islington where Alvina Houghton becomes a nurse: a well-built sandy fellow with a pugnacious face, he is strongly attracted to her. They are like two enemies engaged in a battle: and he is almost a match for her, with his quick, muscular, lambent strength, pitted against her voltaic suddenness of resistance and counter-attack. But by sheer non-human power, electric and paralysing, she overcomes him. *The Lost Girl*

HEATON, MR.: Congregational clergyman who visits Mrs. Morel. He is rather out of place in the mining community, a Cambridge B.A. with 'quaint, fantastic ideas' about the wedding at Cana. 'Poor fellow,' thinks Mrs. Morel, 'his young wife is dead; that is why he makes his love into the Holy Ghost.' Mr. Morel arrives home black from the pit, and embarrasses the timid young clergyman by asking him to feel a miner's sweaty singlet. *Sons and Lovers*

HENRY, MR.: An American guest of Mrs. Norris at Tlacolula—replete with wittily ironical anecdotes demonstrating the absurdities of Mexican politics and of socialism; but who expects to 'turn bolshevist' any day, to save his *pesos. The Plumed Serpent*

HEPBURN, CAPTAIN ALEXANDER: A tall, slender, well-bred Scottish captain, attached to the military in Germany after the war. He has dark eyes, very wide and open; dark hair, parted perfectly on one side, jet-black and glossy, growing grey at the temples; his ankles seem slender and elegant in their fine tartan socks, his brown shoes fit him as if they are part of him. In short, he is exactly like the doll which Hannele makes in imitation of him, and which captivates everyone with its extraordinary likeness: a model of a Scottish soldier in tight-fitting tartan trews, slender and delicately-made, with a slight, elegant stoop of the shoulders; the face beautifully modelled, dark-skinned, with a little, close-cut dark moustache, wide-open dark eyes, and the air of aloofness and of perfect diffidence which marks an officer and a gentleman. Captain Hepburn has an odd way of speaking, as if only half-attending, as if he is really somewhere else. He is the lover of Hannele, a German countess. His superiors are alerted to his involvement with a German national, by the inquisitive, suspicious and interfering Mrs. Hepburn; and they advise him to leave for England. And though he does not want to go, he will not make any declaration to Hannele, nor give any indication as to his plans or intentions. With an incomprehensible, gargoyle smile on his face, a strange, lurking, changeless-seeming grin, his face is like a mask; he has strange, deep-graven lines, a glossy dark skin and a fixed look—as if carved half-grotesquely in some glossy stone, like a Chinese carved soapstone ape. His black hair on his smooth, beautifully shaped head seems changeless. To him words, thoughts, plans, external obligations and responsibilities, mean nothing: so in the complex situation created by his wife's intervention in his affair with Hannele, he is helpless. He simply wants to be together with Hannele, and forget the rest. She insists that he will have to care, to decide, to make up his mind what he wants to do. He just wants to forget, not to bother. However much Hannele presses him, nothing seems to him of any significance. He cannot contemplate the future, he can only live in the present moment; which makes Hannele bitter and unsatisfied—if he doesn't care about the future, then he doesn't care about anything, so how can he care about her? But still, 'the very irrelevancy' of the man overcomes her; the very meaninglessness of him fascinates her and leaves her powerless. When his wife dies after falling from a third-floor hotel window, the Captain feels 'strangely happy' not for himself, but for her sake. It is as if she has been released from some great tension; as if now for the first time she is free. For himself, he feels as if a hatchet has cut through the veins that connect him with other people, the bonds of vital human relationship are severed. The emotional flow between himself and all the people he cares for is broken.

He doesn't even want to see Hannele. He shrinks with a feeling of disgust from his friends and acquaintances, from anyone who offers sympathy or wishes to share emotion. But he is deeply, profoundly thankful that his wife is dead: it means an end of his pity for her. She has gone her own way into the void, like a flown bird. But the convulsion into solitude is followed by a new, growing need to be with someone: though it is not love he desires—not the kind of love he felt for his wife. He will never again go on his knees to adore a woman. He goes back to Munich after an absence abroad, and sees his doll in a shop-window; from there he traces Hannele to a mountain resort in the Tyrol, where she is engaged to marry the Herr Regierungsrat von Poldi. Hannele and the Captain climb a glacier together in the tripper-populated resort: there is now a silent hostility between them. She is thrilled and excited by the high air, the cold, the savage raving of the mountain streams, the awful flanks of livid rock. But he, dark, slender and rather feline, hates it all. 'Wonderful!' cries Hannele; and his reply is 'Yes: and horrible. Detestable.' In opposition to Hannele's admiration, he hates the mountains, for what he calls their 'affectation', their loftiness and uplift; he despises 'people prancing on mountain-tops and feeling exalted'. She looks in wonder at his dark, glowing, ineffectual face, like a dark flame burning in the daylight, in the ice-rains, ineffectual and unnecessary. To him, the mountains are not really bigger than humanity—they are less. Alone, he surmounts the great glacier, and finds himself alone in an intolerable, inhuman, frozen world; he feels the wonder, the terror, and the bitterness of it—'Never a warm leaf to unfold, never a gesture of life to give off. A world sufficient unto itself in lifelessness; all this ice'. The Captain asks Hannele to marry him: but not on a basis of love. He expresses his deep offence that she should have been able to 'make a doll of him'. He wants not to be loved, but to be honoured and obeyed: a woman could love him, and yet still make a doll of him. To her, love is the absolute feeling that comprehends within itself honour and obedience: and to his demands for an oath of fealty she is not disposed to submit. She cannot see herself being a patient Griselda. Yet because she loves him, she half-yields, acquiescent: he remains in his own darkness, unyielding. *The Captain's Doll*

HEPBURN, MRS. (EVANGELINE): Wife of Captain Hepburn; a little lady, with a wrinkled face that still has its crumpled prettiness. She has a very trim figure, bright eyes, a pretty laugh, fine clothes and jewellery, and a rather lardy-dardy middle-class voice. Having heard rumours of her husband's infidelity, she alerts his superiors with the object of stopping the romance. Then she arrives at Hannele's studio, ostensibly to inspect the dolls, but actually to follow up her suspicions that Mitchka is the guilty party—an erroneous suspicion which is only confirmed in Mrs. Hepburn's mind by her introduction to the Captain's doll. She confides in Hannele her conviction that Mitchka is his lover: she believes that the war has had a deteriorating effect upon the morality of Allied menfolk, and they should as far as possible be protected from morally suspect women. She still believes her husband to be kind and considerate, though not perfect, certainly not brutal or cruel—she can magnanimously forgive his 'one little slip', recognising that it is only human to fall in love a little. She musingly recounts, to Hannele's immense embarrassment, detailed romantic experiences from their early marriage—she is playing the heroine in a fantasy romance, the romance of her life. But to Mitchka she is unremittingly hostile, proposing to have her removed by the military authorities. 'I'm the last person in the world to bear malice' she says, in a tone conveying a dire threat. She also demands from Hannele the Captain's doll; which Hannele refuses to part with. After issuing a letter of ultimatum to Hannele, which is forwarded to Alexander, Mrs. Hepburn falls mysteriously from a third-storey window and is killed. *The Captain's Doll*

HERBERTSON, CAPTAIN: One of the few surviving officers of the guards after the war. Good-looking and rather stout. He visits Rawdon Lilly to talk obsessively about the war, in a 'hot, blind, mesmerised voice, mesmerised by a vision that the soul cannot bear'. *Aaron's Rod*

HILL: A boy in Ursula Brangwen's class at Brinsley Street school, poor and rather cunning, pale and colourless, with thin legs knocked at the knees. *The Rainbow*

HODGKISSON, BILL: A friend of Walter Morel's, who gives him a coconut after the Wakes Fair. *Sons and Lovers*

HOLIDAY, MR.: A boarder at the establishment of Siegmund MacNair's widow Beatrice; short and very stout, ruddy with black hair. He has a disagreeable voice, is 'vulgar in the grain', but with a handsome lusty appearance. *The Trespasser*

HOOPER, LADY ARTEMIS: A society lady who has somehow managed to fall through the window of a taxi-cab, and invites Aaron Sisson to soothe her convalescence with music. In her raucous, rasping voice is the 'reckless note of the modern social freebooter'. *Aaron's Rod*

HOUGHTON, ALVINA: A slim girl, rather distinguished in appearance, with her slender face, fine, slightly arched nose, and beautiful, grey-blue eyes, with sardonic, tilting eyelids. She walks with a delicate, lingering motion, and her face looks still. For twenty years she remains the demure, refined creature acceptable to her father and her governess, Miss Frost. But then she rebels, horrifying Manchester House by becoming a maternity nurse. She begins to proceed into knowledge and experience beyond those of Woodhouse: knowledge of 'the human animal, the human organism in its convulsions, the human social beast in its abjection and degradation'. She discovers that life is not all purity and high-mindedness. Somewhere at the back of her mind is the fixed idea or intention of finding love, a man. The craving possesses her and sustains her, darkly and unconsciously. Soon after meeting Cicio she realises that he will triumph over her. She fears that he may be just stupid and bestial; but the dark, other-worldly beauty of his face sends a deep spasm across her. When they become lovers, he casts the powerful, mysterious, horrible spell over her, the spell of his unknown beauty, his darkness and unfathomed handsomeness. Alvina feels herself swept away, away from all other relationships and commitments, away into a 'strange, sleep-like submission to his being'. He takes her to Italy, and for the first time she is spell-bound by the magic of the world itself: 'Whatever life may be, whatever horror men have made of it, the world is a lovely place.' In all the discomfort, poverty and squalor of Cicio's rough, primitive mountain home, Alvina feels 'transfigured' by the new relationship: 'clairvoyant in another mystery of life'. *The Lost Girl*

57

HOUGHTON, CLARISS: Wife of James, mother of Alvina; daughter of a Derbyshire squire, she is courted by James with the expectation of a handsome fortune, an expectation sadly disappointed; he uses her to beget a child, then leaves her alone to her nervous repressions and heart disease. She rapidly becomes an invalid, and dies while Alvina is still a young woman. *The Lost Girl*

HOUGHTON, JAMES: At the age of twenty-eight James inherits a splendid business in Manchester goods; he is then a tall, thin elegant young man, with side-whiskers; 'with a taste for elegant conversation, and elegant literature, and elegant Christianity'; brittle and fluttering, full of facile ideas, and above all a tradesman. But James is also a dreamer, and a kind of commercial poet. He weaves in his imagination an elaborate fantasy of commerce. He dreams of a business purveying beautiful clothes to elegant society ladies—in a colliery town of the Midlands. His goods are in perfect taste, but his customers are in as bad taste as possible, and so James's trade deteriorates into a series of bargain sales. Subsequently his commercial fantasies lead him into a series of disastrous ventures—the Klondyke brickfield, the Throttle Ha'penny pit, and finally the cinema, Houghton's last endeavour. At last the tireless entrepreneur dies, bequeathing to his daughter nothing but debts. *The Lost Girl*

HOUSELEY, MRS.: Landlady of the Royal Oak, sometime lover of Aaron Sisson. She carries her head thrown back with dauntless self-sufficiency, has reddish-brown eyes, and a nose with a subtle, beautiful Hebraic curve. Loudly self-righteous, dangerous, destructive and lustful, she envelops Aaron in the great fierce warmth of her 'female glow'. *Aaron's Rod*

I

INGER, WINIFRED: Ursula's class-mistress; a beautiful woman of twenty-eight; 'a fearless-seeming clean type of modern girl, whose very independence betrays her sorrow.' She is clever, skilled in whatever she does, quick and commanding. With her proud, clear, blue eyes, she gives the impression of 'a fine-mettled, scrupulously-groomed person, with an unyielding mind'. Yet there is an infinite pathos about her, a great poignancy in her lonely, proudly-closed mouth. Ursula forms a lesbian relationship with Winifred, which for a time is life itself to the younger girl. But gradually a nausea comes over her, a 'heavy, clogged sense of deadness'. Ursula begins to reject Winifred: 'the fine, unquenchable flame of the younger girl would consent no more to mingle with the perverted life of the elder woman'. Eventually Winifred marries Tom Brangwen (Junior), Ursula's uncle. *The Rainbow*

INWOOD, THE REVEREND MR.: Clergyman at the Vicarage near the Wookeys' farm; he is the employer of Paula Jablonowsky, the Polish governess who loves Maurice Wooky. A pale, cold man, the vicar hates Paula, who looks after his daughter Marjorie; to both himself and his wife, she is intolerable, like a wild thing, disobedient and insolent. They can hardly wait to get rid of her. *Love Among the Haystacks*

ISABEL, DOÑA: Aunt to Don Ramón Carrasco—she adores him with uncritical, nun-like adoration, worships him with trembling, fearful joy. *The Plumed Serpent*

J

JABLONOWSKY, PAULA: A Polish (or German) girl who looks after the daughter of the Reverend Mr. Inwood. She comes from Hanover, where her father is a shopkeeper; but she ran away from home because she did not like him. She is young, swift and light, with a strange, wild-cat way of grinning; her hair is blonde and full of life, all crisped into many tendrils with vitality, shaking round her face. Her fine blue eyes are peculiarly lidded, and from them she looks now piercingly, now languorously, like a wild cat. She is desired by both Geoffrey and Maurice Wookey, and at first seems attracted to Geoffrey; but then she prefers Maurice. They become lovers and eventually marry. *Love Among the Haystacks*

JAKE, LONG-ARMED: A little square man with long thick arms, half gorilla, half satyr, roaring and booing; an expert in fisticuffs, he brawls amicably with Jack Grant when Jack receives the unsolicited attentions of Jake's girl. *The Boy in the Bush*

JAMES, DR.: Doctor at Islington Maternity Hospital where Alvina Houghton works as a nurse; a quick, slender, dark-haired fellow, a gentleman and immaculately well-dressed, he is always trying to catch Alvina out with his quickness and his exaggerated generosity. *The Lost Girl*

JAMESON, DR.: Friendly, affable, kind and busy doctor who attends Mrs. Morel in her final illness. *Sons and Lovers*

JAZ: *see* Trewhella, William James

JENKINS, JOSHUA: Joiner, carpenter, undertaker, J.P. and coroner as well when required, in the Australian town of York. He takes the measurements of Gran and Jacob Ellis. *The Boy in the Bush*

JENNIE: A 'common' girl picked up by Will Brangwen in a music hall in Nottingham; the object of his sensual attentions. *The Rainbow*

JESÚS: Elder son of Juana, Kate Leslie's housekeeper; a queer, heavy, greasy fellow, who runs the electricity generating plant and does odd jobs. *The Plumed Serpent*

JIM: A labourer on the Wookeys' farm. *Love Among the Haystacks*

JIMINEZ, BISHOP OF THE WEST: A thin old man with an affable manner and suspicious looks. An official of the orthodox Catholic Church, he responds rather unsympathetically to the announcement that Don Ramón, backed up by Cipriano's storm-troopers, proposes to remove the Christian images from the church of Sayula, replacing them with Aztec idols. *The Plumed Serpent*

JIMMY: Eyeglass-screwing friend of Lady Artemis Hooper. *Aaron's Rod*

JOAN: Friend of Madeleine and the mother of the man who died, and his former follower; the three women seek him near the empty tomb, but he has no wish to enter again into connection. *The Man who Died*

JONES, MR.: Sub-postmaster at Chomesbury (Shropshire), a man of forty-five, thick-set, with a foolish complexion and foolish brown eyes. He unctuously delivers a telegram to Lou Carrington, to the accompaniment of a gorgeous bow and a fatuous smile. *St. Mawr*

JORDAN, THOMAS: Manufacturer, owner of 'Thomas Jordan and Sons, Surgical Appliances' where Paul Morel takes a situation as a clerk. A red-faced, white-whiskered old man, who reminds Paul of a Pomeranian dog. He is snappy and business-like, quite a gentleman, but feels the need to play the role of proprietor. *Sons and Lovers*

JOSÉ: (Appears posthumously). The German-Mexican son of the owner of the lakeside hotel at Orilla where Kate Leslie stays; in the course of a robbery he is hacked to death by Indian machetes. *The Plumed Serpent*

JUANA: Kate Leslie's housekeeper and general servant: a short woman of forty, with a full, dark face, centreless dark eyes, untidy hair and a limping walk. A sloven, she is the mother, by various fathers, of Jesús, Ezequiel, Concha and Maria. She combines the deep-rooted hostility and 'bottom-dog insolence' of the Mexican Indian, with sudden touches of passionate warmth, and the 'peculiar selfless generosity of the natives'. *The Plumed Serpent*

JULIO: A bricklayer who comes to stay with his cousin Juana, bringing his wife Maria del Carmen. *The Plumed Serpent*

K

KANGAROO: *see* Cooley, Benjamin

KIRK, MRS.: The Morels' next-door neighbour, who assists Mrs. Morel in her labour when Paul is born. *Sons and Lovers*

KIRK, MRS.: A stout, pale, sharp-nosed woman, sly, with something shrewish and cat-like underneath; she nursed Gerald

Crich as a child, and describes to Gudrun Brangwen how wilful and masterful he was as a baby, and with what relish she was wont to 'pinch his little bottom for him'. *Women in Love*

KIRK, TOM: One of the miners who gather for 'intellectual discussion' at the Royal Oak; a man with a sharp sense of humour. *Aaron's Rod*

L

LAW, MAJOR: American military attaché in Mexico, a guest of Mrs. Norris at Tlacolula. In company with all the other *gringos*, he despises post-revolutionary Mexico. *The Plumed Serpent*

LAWSON, MRS.: A woman over fifty, a friend of Miss Frost, and a tearful celebrant of her departed friend's magnificent and life-long self-sacrifice. *The Lost Girl*

LEDERMAN: The husband of 'the woman who rides away'. Twenty years older than she is, he is a little, wiry, twisted fellow, with brown, greying hair. He has made his fortune in silver-mining by his own energy—he has made himself by making his circumstances. They have two children, a boy Freddy and a girl Margarita, who mean little to either parent. At fifty-three, he is still as tough and tenacious as wire, and full of energy: but the post-war decline in the silver-market, by diminishing his activity, dims and diminishes his personal self. He is a good man, and a good husband; and he loves his wife—never quite getting over his dazzled admiration of her. But in himself he remains essentially a bachelor: he is primarily the boss of his industry, and his marriage is the last and most intimate section of his 'works'. He cherishes and admires his wife as he cherishes and admires his mine: and he jealously guards her in the same possessive way. To her he never actually becomes real, either mentally or physically—but morally he keeps her in absolute, invincible slavery. He is really a squeamish idealist, who hates the physical side of life; but he loves work, making things, and making things go. His marriage and his children are an extension of his productive activity: and his profits on that particular investment come in the form of sentiment and the illusion of conjugal bliss. He loves to invite white gentlemen, young mining engineers, to his house, enjoying their company; but his wife too is fascinated, and he is really an old-fashioned miner—for a man to admire his wife is like a precious vein of silver being looted in his mine. So he keeps her at home as a closely guarded secret; until, during his absence on business, she finally rebels and rides away across the mountains. *The Woman who Rode Away*

LEDERMAN, MRS.: 'The woman who rides away'. She is disillusioned with her marriage, which she had expected to be an adventure—even though her husband is distinguished more by his accomplishments than in himself. At thirty-three, she is a large, blue-eyed, dazed woman, beginning to grow stout: in character she has never really developed beyond the rather dazzling Californian girl from Berkeley; her conscious development was arrested on her marriage. Then an interest, a fascination, begins to stir within her for the stories of the Indians who live beyond the mountains: their savage customs, their wild ways, their ancient religious beliefs; a peculiar, vague enthusiasm for unknown Indians finds a full echo in her woman's heart—she is overcome by 'a foolish romanticism more unreal than a girl's'. She feels it her destiny to ride away, across the secret mountains, into the mysterious haunts of the timeless, eternal Indians. One tribe especially captivates her imagination, the Chilchuis; the sacred tribe of all the Indians, descendants of the old Aztec kings, who are said still to offer human sacrifice. So in her husband's absence she makes her 'crazy plans', to ride away in search of the legendary Chilchuis—to be free. The large, seemingly placid, fair-complexioned woman is determined to have her way: she treats the objections of her house-servant Manuel with peculiar, overbearing emphasis. In the wild, savage mountain country, the feeling of loneliness is an elation to her, like a drink of cold water to one who is thirsty. She is not even afraid, but buoyed up with a curious, bubbling elation. In the cold starlight she feels like a woman who has died and passed beyond. In the curious receptivity of her new-born self, in the exhaustion of the journey, in the lightheadedness caused by the high mountain air, she nears her destination rather vague and disheartened—if she had any will left, she would turn back, to the security and protection of her home, husband and family. But she has lost her will. Then she is confronted by three of the Chilchui Indians, dark-faced, strongly-built men in dark serapes and straw hats. She deals with them instinctively as she would her husband's servants; a faint smile of assurance on her face, a half-childish, half-arrogant confidence in her own female power and her social superiority: the assurance of her own white womanhood. The young Indian who speaks to her has quick, large, bright black eyes glancing sideways; a soft black moustache and sparse tufts of beard; long black hair full of life, hanging unrestrained on his shoulders. Her attempts to command the men meet with a strangely impersonal indifference: looking into their black eyes, her spirit quails—they are not human to her, as if she were some strange thing. All the anger of a spoilt white woman rises in her against these anonymous, dark-faced men: but this has no effect on their snake-like eyes, bright with derision. Under their indifferent, impersonal control, she is powerless, supremely angry, but also exultant. She knows she is dead. The Indians do not attempt to harm or even touch her: they merely look at her with an intense, remote, inhuman glitter: because of her whiteness, they do not really see her as a woman. At the Chilchui village she is brought before the elders, resplendent in red and orange, yellow and black serapes, and brilliant feathered headdresses. She is examined by the chief, father of the young Indian, an old man with a lined, wrinkled face the colour of dark bronze: he scrutinises her with eyes of piercing strength, and without misgiving in their demonish, dauntless power. His gaze is inhuman, looking into her past, her resistance and her challenge, into she knows not what. Asked why she has come, she replies that she has abandoned the white man's god, and comes to seek the god of the Chilchuis. When her answer is translated to the listening Indians, a thrill of triumph and exultance can be felt rippling through the tense silence; and they stare at her with a steely glitter of covetousness—not desire, but an impersonal, abstract, religious satisfaction. She feels no fear: fear has died with her old self. She feels merely a 'cold, watchful wonder'.

She is taken to see an ancient, dying elder of the tribe, the former chief, grandfather to the young Indian who first spoke to her: an old man with snow-white hair, remote as a ghost, his face almost black, with a far-off, other-wordly intentness. His black eyes look at her as if from the dead, seeing the unseen. They remove her clothes and inspect her, without desire on their part or shame on hers: they are only dark and tense with some other, deep, gloomy, incomprehensible emotion; while the young Indian has a strange look of ecstasy on his face. She feels no particular shame, as if her body is not her own. They dress her in new clothing, and imprison her in a stockade. The young Indian comes to her, very gentle and thoughtful, and on his face the look of triumph and ecstasy: in his black eyes, with their curving dark lashes, a strange soft glow of ecstasy, quite impersonal, not really human. She is treated with drugs, which soothe her with languor, her limbs feel loose and languid, her sensations acute and heightened, keen, distinct and vivid; as if all her senses are so diffused on the air that she can hear the evening flowers unfolding, and hear the crystal sounds of the heavens in motion. All the Indians treat her with gentleness and fatherly solicitude: but lurking in their dark eyes she glimpses something awesomely ferocious and relentless, which gives her a shock of fear. The young Indian is her most constant visitor: the grandson of the old chief and son of the present chief, he will be the tribe's Cacique. As he sits with her she observes his broad, powerful shoulders, the blackish, heavy lips, and feels his dark and powerful maleness. And yet he sits with her for hours, without any sex-consciousness between them. As the days go by, she sometimes feels a touch of horror at her loss of power and control: but the Indians cast their spell over her, leaving her will-less. In the savage, rhythmic dancing and singing of the Indians, she recognises the death of her own kind of womanhood, intensely personal and individual, sharp and quivering in nerve-consciousness; the obliteration of the highly-bred white woman's self-consciousness, and its merging into 'the great stream of impersonal sex and impersonal passion'. The sacrifice prepares. The young Indian speaks to her of their beliefs and their mythology: the Chilchuis hold that the sun and the moon are the principles of manhood and womanhood, and that men should possess the power of the sun and women that of the moon. But the power of the sun has passed away from the Red men to the White men, who do not know how to use its power; and the power of the moon has passed away to the white woman, who does not know how to use it. The white woman must be sacrificed to the sun, and then the sun and moon will return to the Indians. She knows she is going to die, among the glistening snow of this high mountain world, at the hands of this savage, sumptuous people. As she feels dead already, the transition from life to death seems easy and unimportant. She is sacrificed as the rays of the setting sun penetrate deep into the sacred cave of the Chilchuis. The old priests watch the sun in sightless concentration, seeing beyond the sun; and in their black, empty concentration she sees intense power, deep as the earth's heart, deep as the heart of the sun. By the sacrifice of the woman they achieve power: 'The mastery that man must hold, and that passes from race to race.' *The Woman who Rode Away*

LEITNER: Love-companion and penniless dependant of Loerke: large and fair, handsome enough in his uneasy, slightly abject fashion, with humility that seems to cover some kind of fear. *Women in Love*

LEIVERS, AGATHA: Elder sister of Miriam, a school-teacher. Fair and small and determined, she has rebelled against the dominant values of her home and against the doctrine of the other cheek. Out in the world and becoming independent, she insists on wordly values of appearance, manner and position. *Sons and Lovers*

LEIVERS, EDGAR: Miriam's brother; rather small, rather formal for a farmer, with a certain 'brutality of manner'; but partly educated, a rationalist who has a curious, scientific interest in life. Like his brother Maurice, he finds it difficult to establish with outsiders anything like 'ordinary human feeling'—they are always restless for something deeper, yearning for soul-intimacy. Edgar is Paul Morel's 'very close friend'. *Sons and Lovers*

LEIVERS, HUBERT: The youngest Leivers child, fawned and drooled over with passionate intensity by his sister Miriam. *Sons and Lovers*

LEIVERS, MIRIAM: The boyhood sweetheart and eventual lover of Paul Morel. Brown-eyed and dark-haired, Miriam is intensely romantic, in her imagination a princess turned into a swine girl. Her life is all imagination, mysticism and religion, and she recoils from the vulgarity, the commonness, the drudgery of her ordinary life. She is exceedingly sensitive, and the slightest physical grossness makes her recoil in anguish. She seems always like a maiden in bondage in some dreamy tale, 'her spirit dreaming in a land far away and magical'. For Miriam, all experiences must be kindled in her imagination before she feels she possesses them; her intensity is incapable of accepting emotion on a normal plane—everything about her is 'gripped stiff' with intensity, and the effort, overcharged, recoils on itself. She loves Paul absorbedly, with a clinging affection; she desires always to embrace him, but only in so far as he does not want her physically. To Paul it seems that she never realises *him*, that he could be a mere object to her—that she never appreciates or understands the male that he is. She prefers instead to create moments of intense emotional communion with Paul, especially in relation to nature, in which she experiences little stillnesses of ecstasy; but Paul remains detached and uncomfortable. Eventually she relinquishes herself to him sexually, but as a sacrifice in which she feels something of horror. Her soul stands apart. 'She lay to be sacrificed because she loved him so much. And he had to sacrifice her'. When Paul breaks off their relationship she is hurt, but almost glad: she had always felt in a kind of bondage to him, which she hated because she could not control it. 'Deep down, she had hated him, because she loved him, and he dominated her.' *Sons and Lovers*

LEIVERS, MRS: Mother of Edgar, Miriam, Agatha, Geoffrey, Maurice and Hubert; like Miriam she is intense and religious; she exalts everything—even a bit of housework—to the plane of a religious trust, and sticks unflinchingly to the doctrine of 'the other cheek'. With Miriam she 'kindles' Paul Morel to his creative work. *Sons and Lovers*

LENSKY, ANNA: *see* Brangwen, Anna

LENSKY, LYDIA: *see* Brangwen, Lydia

LEONARD: A friend of Paul Morel and Miriam Leivers; a

'comic, thin fellow', he marries Annie Morel. *Sons and Lovers*

LESLIE, KATE: Née Forrester, formerly Tylor; forty-year-old widow of the Irish political leader James Joachim Leslie; a beautiful woman in an unconventional way, with soft brown hair and hazel eyes and a beautiful, distant repose. She watches people as if she were reading a novel, with detached, disinterested amusement. She never really belongs to any society—too Irish, too wise. In England, in Europe, Kate has heard the *consummatum est* of her own spirit; the flow of her life has broken, and she cannot restart it in Europe. She recoils absolutely from the modern world and all its values; she no longer yearns for the love of man, or even the love of her children: the craving for companionship, sympathy, love has left her. 'Something infinitely intangible but infinitely blessed took its place: a peace that passes understanding.' But she continues to oppose and struggle against the 'powerful, degenerate thing called *life*', and to seek for the reality of a true loneliness, 'the influx of peace and soft, flower-like potency that was beyond understanding'. And so she is in Mexico: and in the Mexican *peons* she finds something—they are able to touch her with a fire of compassion, they seem to afford the possibility of new relationships; a 'communion of grace'. She finds it also in Don Ramón, and in her half-reluctant participation in the mysteries and rituals of Quetzalcoatl. But above all in Cipriano she finds the supreme male power, the primeval phallic mystery of the twilit, primitive world—godlike, demonic power in a living man: 'The Master: the Everlasting Pan'. Cipriano is the answer to her prayer: 'Give me the mystery, and let the world live again for me! And deliver me from man's automatism!' Kate marries Cipriano, and becomes a goddess in their private pantheon—the bride of Huitzilopochtli, the first flower of Quetzalcoatl—and takes the Aztec name of Malintzi. Despite this, she plans to return to Europe: but the gods of Mexico, Ramón-Quetzalcoatl and Cipriano-Huitzilopochtli, hold her irresistibly: 'you won't let me go!' *The Plumed Serpent*

LEVISON: An acquaintance of James Argyle in Florence, still young and callow enough to cherish the illusion of 'fair play'. *Aaron's Rod*

LEWIS, AMOS and EMMA: Servants of the old John Grant, they are nearly as crazy as he is. *The Boy in the Bush*

LEWIS, MORGAN: St. Mawr's Welsh groom; a little, quick, rather bow-legged, loosely built fellow, with a little black beard and phosphorescent pale grey eyes, like the eyes of an animal peering from under a bush. He is the stallion's 'attendant shadow', and cares about nothing in the world except, at the present, St. Mawr. People do not matter to him. Lewis appears unusual in that he has never wanted a home, a wife and children, or any real connection with other human beings—only his relationship with the horse is life to him. At one moment when he and Mrs. Witt are fleeing with St. Mawr, Lewis drops his stony, inaccessible pride, and loquaciously and naively describes his belief in ancient superstitions, fairies and nature-spirits. But when Mrs. Witt responds to this by offering herself in marriage, he congeals again into his cold, proud anger and his fierce, resentful chastity: 'No woman shall touch my body, and mock and despise me. No woman.' *St. Mawr*

LIBIDNIKOV, MAXIM: A prim young Russian friend of Julius Halliday, with a smooth, warm-coloured face, and black, oiled hair; dark, smooth-skinned, full of stealthy vigour, and with a whispering, gentlemanly voice. *Women in Love*

LILY: A half-cast girl, big as a coal-barge, who sits aggressively forward with elbows and wrists much in evidence, and her pleasant swarthy face alight with eager anticipation, as the massed Ellises play 'Modern Proposals'. Easu wins the contest with his laconic proposal to her: 'Hump y'r bluey and come home.' *The Boy in the Bush*

LILLY, RAWDON: A writer, a little, dark, thin, quick fellow. His life is dominated by two impulses: the impulse to remain himself, to 'pivot himself on his own pride', to 'possess his own soul, in patience, and peace, and isolation'; and the impulse to go out to others, to help and comfort, to care and love. The only solution to this dilemma lies in forcing those he helps to accept his predominance and superiority, so he can turn to others without breaking his individual integrity. Lilly's philosophy is that man is essentially alone—'the heart beats alone in its silence'. Aaron Sisson recognises that Lilly *is* intrinsically alone, and that this isolation and self-sufficiency guarantee his reality. Aaron feels that Lilly is *there*, clearly existing in life, but without asking for or preventing connections with others. He knows that he can depend on Lilly for help, even for life itself—'so long as it entailed no breaking of the intrinsic isolation of Lilly's soul'. *Aaron's Rod*

LILLY, TANNY: Rawdon Lilly's wife: a fine Norwegian blonde, rather like Frieda Lawrence. *Aaron's Rod*

LIMB, EMMIE: Childhood friend of the Morel children. *Sons and Lovers*

LINDLEY, THE REVEREND ERNEST: Vicar of Aldecross, father of Mary, Louisa, Sidney, etc. As a young man he comes from Cambridge and a curacy in Suffolk to take charge of an obsolete church in a raw colliery district of the Midlands, where with the help of his self-assured young wife he hopes to keep up a superior position. Unfortunately the raw, disaffected colliers refuse to acknowledge any such superiority—they are cheerfully contemptuous and good-humouredly indifferent. At first indignant, then tacitly resentful, he is gradually reduced to conscious hatred of his 'flock'. He is without character, dependent upon his position in society to give him status among men. Now in poverty and without social standing, without any instinct of sociability, and without any individual strength of assertion, he drags on, pale and miserable and neutral. His life is spent haggling to make ends meet, and bitterly repressing and pruning his children into gentility, urging them to ambition, weighting them with duty. The vicar supports and encourages Mary's marriage to the physically repulsive but financially independent Mr. Massy; but disapproves strongly of Louisa's genuinely loving marriage to the young collier Alfred Durant. He advises them to move as far as possible away from the district, to protect his precious 'position'. *The Daughters of the Vicar*

LINDLEY, LOUISA: The second child of The Reverend Edward Lindley; short and plump, rather plain, obstinate-looking, with a heavy jaw, a proud brow, and grey brooding eyes, very beautiful when she smiles. Miss Louisa does not share her sister Mary's admiration of the Reverend Mr. Massy, the wealthy but dwarfish clergyman: she can only regard the ugly little man with aversion, dislikes him exceedingly, and would like to see him annihilated. But in her conscience, a sense of 'deeper justice' makes her feel humble before her sister. When, in company with Mr. Massy, Louisa visits the dying Mr. Durant, she recognises the justice and moral power of her feelings, in her fear and distaste for the dispassionate, emotionless clergyman, and her corresponding attraction to Alfred Durant, absorbed in his natural, spontaneous grief for his father. She remembers him vividly in the sickroom, embracing his mother, his voice broken with grief and tenderness; his ruddy face and golden-brown eyes, kind and careless, but now strained with a natural fear. It goes through her like a flame of pride, to think of his figure, like 'a straight, fine jet of life'. Alfred remains separate from her, avoiding connection, putting himself in the role of an inferior; but her fierce, obstinate heart 'clings to its own rights', and will not give way. She will not submit to the calm placing of her as an inaccessible superior—the sentient woman who is fond of him resists the impersonal, divisive separation of class. After Mary's marriage to Mr. Massy, Louisa's being rebels: Mary, her ideal of good Christian living, becomes subject to question—how can one be pure in thought and spirit, and yet subject oneself to a situation which is physically degrading and repulsive? Louisa demands love, and she will have it— irrespective of money, social position, respectability, the real gods of her father's world. Such a belief naturally makes her isolated and set apart in the vicarage: but she is obstinate and unyielding. Irritated to extremity by Mr. Massy's fixed, inexorable solicitude, Louisa wanders to Alfred's house at Old Aldecross, and finds Mrs. Durant badly injured. Looking after the sick woman, Louisa participates in the everyday life of a collier's cottage, feeding and washing and caring for Alfred. Despite her misgivings at the almost repulsive physical intimacy and contact, the 'commonness', she discovers in Alfred's body something more real than money, position, social power—a living centre, an intimate personal being, which she can love. *The Daughters of the Vicar*

LINDLEY, MARY: The eldest of the Lindley children, a long slim thing with a fine profile, and a proud, pure look of submission to a higher fate. Like all the Lindley children, she is healthy, but unwarmed and rather rigid: made very proud and genteel, forced rigidly into the mould of the upper class, kept isolated from the common people around. Mary has to work as a governess to a few daughters of small tradespeople. Her heart is chilled and hardened with fear of the perpetual, cold penury, the narrow struggle, the nothingness of their lives. When the Reverend Mr. Massy arrives in Aldecross as a curate and a potential suitor, Miss Mary is repelled by his physical nonentity, respects his wealth, and is forced to honour and admire his inhuman, mechanical goodness and kindness. She forces herself, shuddering yet desirous, to serve him. She is at once cold with admiration for him, and yet touched with pity. But Mr. Massy is stronger, and she knows she must submit to what he is. Although her physical being is prouder and stronger than his, she is in the grip of his moral, mental being; she knows what will happen, and is resigned to it. When Mr. Massy proposes to her, she is stiff with apprehension, but her spirit quivers and waits, while her body goes cold and impervious as stone. While her natural resistance is not strong enough, her parents are delighted with the prospect of such a good and profitable match. In marriage to Mr. Massy Mary tries to become a pure reason, without impulse or feeling; like him she shuts herself up from the agonies of shame and violation which assail her. She *will* not feel; she will be a pure will, acquiescing in him. And by renouncing her body and ignoring the voice of her blood, she achieves a kind of freedom—the freedom of a pure, mental, spiritual will, existing in a welcome state of financial independence. She compensates for her feelings of personal shame and revulsion by the gratification of pride, status, and superiority. Still the voice of the murdered body occasionally speaks, when she feels like annihilating and destroying everything; and when she becomes pregnant, she is filled with horror, afraid before God and man. The baby is a bonny, healthy boy, and his presence almost reawakens in her the physical life she has trampled and extinguished. But to love now is too cruel and racking an effort; as a mother she becomes amorphous, fragmentary, purposeless. While Mary was always to her sister Louisa a model of goodness and spiritual purity, after her marriage to Mr. Massy she becomes another kind of example—moving Louisa strongly to ignore the claims of wealth and status, and to seek genuine human love and affection. *The Daughters of the Vicar*

LINDLEY, MRS.: Wife of The Reverend Ernest Lindley, who marries her as a self-assured young woman, daughter of a Cambridgeshire rector. Finding herself a vicar's wife, in an impoverished position without status, faced with the frank contempt of the local population, she rages with mortification, affects airs and takes a high hand; but without financial backing, her attempts to impress are met with callous ridicule. She discovers herself isolated and wounded to the quick of her pride; her public rages meeting with nothing but contempt, she confines her anger to the home and to herself. Then for fear that her rage and frustration might shatter the form of their life, she goes quiet, bitter and beaten by fear. She produces a child regularly every year, mechanically performing her maternal duty. Gradually, broken by the effort of suppressing her violent anger and misery and disgust, she becomes an invalid, and takes to her couch. When the stunted and inhuman Mr. Massy arrives as curate and as a potential suitor for one of her daughters, Mrs. Lindley finds him physically repulsive and socially intolerable—'What a little abortion!'—but at the back of her mind she sees him as a 'prospect', an unattached gentleman with a solid income. Financial stability is the dominant concern—the man is 'a trifle thrown in'. Naturally Louisa's desire to marry the young collier Alfred Durant meets with Mrs. Lindley's scathing contempt and vulgar, mercenary disapproval. *The Daughters of the Vicar*

LINLEY, MR.: General colliery manager in Clifford Chatterley's mines. *Lady Chatterley's Lover*

LOERKE: A sculptor, a thin, dark-skinned man with quick, full eyes like a mouse's; an odd, detached creature, like a child or a troll; the movement of his mature, sardonic voice has the flexibility of essential energy, and of a mocking penetrating understanding. When Gudrun Brangwen is drifting apart from Gerald, she is intrigued by Loerke: she sees in his eyes 'a black look of inorganic misery'; they are the eyes of a lost being, with a strange, dumb, depraved knowledge, and a spark of uncanny fire. He seems to understand Gudrun with a subconscious, sinister knowledge, devoid of all hope and illusion; and to Gudrun he is the rock-bottom of all life, dispensing with all illusion, caring about nothing, existing as a 'pure unconnected will, stoical and momentaneous.' To Birkin he is a 'rat in the river of corruption'—'a gnawing little negation, gnawing at the roots of life.' *Women in Love*

LOUIE: *see* Travers, Louie

LOUIS: A Swiss Frenchman, moderately tall, with prominent cheekbones, and a wing of glossy black hair falling on his temples; a member of the Natcha-Kee-Tawara travelling theatrical troupe. *The Lost Girl*

LOUISA: A friend of Helena Verden; she feels for Helena an excessive affection, which is a burden to both of them. She is full of small affectations, being consumed with uneasy love. *The Trespasser*

LOVERSEED, MR.: Vicar of Cossethay. *The Rainbow*

LUPE: Kate Leslie's manservant; Kate sees in him the 'eternal child', the savage man, innocent in the fullness of sex. *The Plumed Serpent*

LUPTON: Bridegroom of Laura Crich, a clean-shaven naval man. *Women in Love*

LYSIPPUS: A slave belonging to the mother of the Priestess of Isis, who is involved in the plot to arrest and bring to justice the man who died. *The Man who Died*

M

MABEL: Maidservant of the Carringtons', who offers Fanny some tart advice on how to deal with soft-footed, creeping Indians. *St. Mawr*

MACKINNON, DANNY: In the little Australian town of Paddy's Crossing, Danny Mackinnon stands bursting with wrathful indignation, waiting to marry his daughter to Patrick O'Burk; in a moth-eaten scarlet coat, and overall trousers, top-boots slashed for his bunions, and a forage cap slashed for his increased head, scarlet in the face and bulging out of his youthful uniform. Unfortunately the ceremony is delayed by the arrival of Miss Mackinnon's baby. *The Boy in the Bush*

MACNAIR, BEATRICE: The wife of Siegmund; a woman of good family, brought up like a lady, educated in a convent school in France; but now a slattern and a drudge, slovenly and neglected. When her husband Siegmund leaves for his holiday with Helena, Beatrice lies seething in her impotence, 'discarded like a worn-out object, stiff with bitterness'. On his return she keeps her anger and resentment restrained until it gives way to an outburst of vindictive hysteria, which is met by Siegmund's obstinacy, and the stillness of his white-hot wrath. Beatrice is careful not to let the blow of Siegmund's death fall with full impact upon her. She dodges it. She is afraid to meet the accusation of the dead Siegmund, 'with the sacred jury of memories. When the event summoned her to stand before the bench of her own soul's understanding, she fled, leaving the verdict upon herself entirely suspended.' *The Trespasser*

MACNAIR, FRANK: The son of Siegmund, a tall, thin lad of eighteen. He is filled with contempt for his father after his temporary desertion, judging him insolently and inexorably: 'The damned coward! He *would* come slinking back in a funk!' On his father's death Frank as a sentimentalist weeps over the situation, not the personae. With him, as with the others, the memory of Siegmund begins rapidly to fade. *The Trespasser*

MACNAIR, GWEN: On his return from the Isle of Wight Siegmund hopes to find Gwen, his favourite daughter, his five-year-old girl, 'full of love' for him; he hopes to be able to 'hide his face against her', that she may sleep in his arms. But under her mother's influence Gwen is suspicious and constrained, and turns away from him. *The Trespasser*

MACNAIR, IRENE and MARJORY: Daughters of Siegmund and Beatrice. *The Trespasser*

MACNAIR, SIEGMUND: A handsome man in the prime of life, with dark, tender eyes and a youthful mouth; his hair

75

brushed back from his fine brow; his nose shapely, his chin beautifully moulded. A musician, violinist in a London orchestra. Siegmund is weary of his marriage to Beatrice, and about to spend a week on the Isle of Wight with his lover Helena Verden. It is one of the crises of his life. For years he has suppressed his soul in mechanical despair, doing his duty and enduring. Now 'his soul had been softly enticed from its bondage. Now he was going to break free altogether ...' Siegmund is above all a romantic: he wants to blind himself with Helena, to blaze up all his past and future in a passion worth years of living. But he recognises that 'living too intensely kills you'; that the pattern of his life, the pattern of his finely-wrought fate, is 'love, the brief ecstasy, and the end.' Life with his family and without Helena appears unreal and impossible, absurd and insufferable; a degrading humiliation. 'There remained only one door he could open in this prison corridor of life.' With exact and methodical despair, Siegmund hangs himself. 'He was sure of a wonderful kindness in death. Therefore he could submit and have faith. There was no futile hesitation between doom and pity.' *The Trespasser*

MACNAIR, VERA: Eldest daughter of Siegmund, a rather handsome girl, who greets her father's return with scornful restraint and withering contempt; meanwhile trying to comfort her mother with chattering, affected brightness. When her father is dead, Vera is too practical minded and has too inflexible a moral judgement, ever to put herself in his place, and try to understand him. *The Trespasser*

MACWHIRTER, MR.: A boarder at the establishment of Siegmund MacNair's widow Beatrice: tall, fair and stoutish, quietly spoken, humorous and amiable, yet extraordinarily learned. *The Trespasser*

MADELEINE: The man who died, returning to his empty tomb, finds Madeleine hovering before the entrance, peering into the darkness, wringing her hands and weeping. She wants the man to come back as he was, as teacher and saviour: the need for excessive giving is still strong within her, and she wishes to serve him; her face is dense with need for salvation from the woman she has been, the female who caught men at her will. But the man who died wants no more service, and self-sacrifice. *The Man who Died*

MADEMOISELLE: Governess of Winifred Crich. *Women in Love*

MAJOR, THE: Tall, thin and Oxford-looking, with a black eyepatch, a guest of Sir William Franks at Novara. *Aaron's Rod*

MALINTZI: Aztec name given to Kate Leslie when she is invited to become a goddess by courtesy of Cipriano-Huitzilopochtli. *The Plumed Serpent*

MAN WHO DIED, THE: The man who died awakens in his tomb, numb, cold and full of hurt. He does not want to awaken, to come back from the dead: the strange, incalculable birth of consciousness causes him deep nausea and resistance. Unwilling and loath, the movement of life within him yet forces him to break his cerements with his sore, pierced hands. Arousing to the pitch dark of the tomb, an anguish of imprisonment moves him to escape, to roll away the stone, to confront the piercing keenness of daybreak's sharp breath. Leaving the tomb, he is alone: 'and having died, is even beyond loneliness'; walking forth, wrapped in his shroud, stepping painfully, wincing on his scarred feet over the rocky ground of the garden. Surrounded by the thronging greenness of the natural world from which he had died, he is neither living nor dead, neither of this world nor the next. Looking at him, the peasant sees the dead-white face of an awakened corpse, with the black beard growing on it as if in death; the wide-open, black, sombre eyes that have died; the washed scars on the waxy forehead. The man feels beneath his feet the cool silkiness of the young wheat, sees the buds of the scarlet anenome, and becomes aware of a world of life which has never died, but from which he departed; and now all that remains to him is fathomless disillusion. Invited to stay in his house by the peasant, he eats and drinks, because life must be, although desire is dead within him, even for food and drink. Yet even deeper than his negation and disillusion there is a desireless resoluteness and determination. As he lies in the peasant's yard, he watches the cock, crying out in the necessity to live, even to cry out the triumph of life. Looking around him at life, he sees everywhere a vast resoluteness flinging

77

itself up into wave-crests, like the black and orange cock, glowing with desire and assertion. The destiny of life seems to him more fierce and compulsive than the destiny of death. Why should men be lifted up from this natural world? He was wrong to interfere. 'I have survived the day and the death of my interference, and am still a man.' The teacher and the saviour are dead in him, and now he can grow into his own single life. 'I have not risen from the dead in order to seek death again.' He realises that the body has its own greater life: that chastity is a kind of greed, and that the body rises again to take and to give, ungreedily. He has risen for the woman who knows the greater life of the body. As he moves through the phenomenal world, he recognises the universal mania of compulsion; everyone, in a mad assertion of ego, wants to place compulsion over others. His own mission now seems on reflection to have been the same thing: to lay the compulsion of love on all men and all things. He has come back to life, but not the life he had left, of little people and the little day. Now he is alone and apart from others, seeking the fulfilment of his own life. This he finds in the young Priestess of Isis, who sees him as the lost Osiris, risen from death, to be made whole again. Shall he give himself to her touch? She is a tender flower of healing, more terrible and lovely than the death he died. The woman of Isis is lovely to him, not so much in form, as in the womanly glow of her: a potent woman, to touch her is like touching the sun. He discovers himself erect and risen in the flesh, to desire and fulfilment, to the poignancy of wonder and the marvellous, piercing transcendence of desire; to the deep, interfolded, penetrable warmth of a woman. But the Priestess's mother and the slaves, those who still live the petty little jealous life of the little day, want to prevent their fulfilment. So he goes, having sown the seed of his life and his resurrection, and put his touch upon the choicest woman of his day. *The Man who Died*

MANBY, FLORA: Rico's floral and roseate girl-friend, who is jolly well glad she lives in 1920-odd, and not at some perfectly beastly time in the past when women had to cringe before mouldy domineering men. She is a brick, a topping good sport. *St. Mawr*

MARASCA, FRANCESCO: *see* Cicio

MARCH, ELLEN (NELLIE): The more robust of the two girls who work Bailey Farm; she is 'the man about the place'. She has learned carpentry and joinery at evening classes in Islington; she does most of the outdoor work; in her puttees and breeches, her belted coat and her loose cap, she looks almost like a graceful young man, her shoulders straight, her movements easy and confident. But her face is not a man's face. Her eyes are big and wide and dark, strange, startled and shy, but also a little sardonic. Her mouth is pinched as if in pain and irony. But there is an almost satirical flash to her eyes, and a slight, dangerous satire in her voice. She is a creature of odd whims and unsatisfied tendencies. March is strangely moved by the presence of the fox, who prowls about the farm stealing chickens: one full, mellow August evening, as she keeps sentinel in her constant state of musing abstraction, her eyes keen and observant, her soul remote and rapt and absorbed, the fox appears before her—and as they exchange glances, a kind of recognition takes place. He makes off, with casual arrogance, secure in his own power, indifferent to March's affected manliness. March is determined to find him; mindless and spellbound she seeks him. She is possessed by him, by his dark, shrewd, unabashed eye, by his easy mastering of her spirit, his contempt and his cunning. For months, whenever she falls into her half-musing unconsciousness, the fox dominates her, comes over her like a spell. When Henry the young soldier unobtrusively asserts himself into their life, March recognises him as the fox: although she screws up her mouth in tight primness, striving to keep her will in control, still she feels the soft, vibrating running of his voice, her eyes dilate and glow, she loses herself. She shrinks from his steady, penetrating gaze, holds her face averted, tries to disappear. But his eyes follow her with searching, unremitting, fixed attention. As he talks to Banford, March watches him, and feels the fox in full presence. Now she can feel peaceful, she need not seek him any more; she yields to the subtle animal spell, lapses into the odour of the fox. At night she dreams of the fox, singing round the house, moving her to tears; she feels with pain and wonder his beauty, his dangerousness, his vicious animal nature. When Henry asks to marry her, she reacts with startled suspicion and fear, but at

79

the same time a great relaxation comes over her; she struggles to maintain her own power, but in herself she swoons dimly into unconscious acquiescence under his soft, heavy insistence. Although March is held closely by Banford, when Henry shoots the fox her fate seems to become clear: she dreams Banford is dead, and that she lays in her coffin wrapped in a fox-skin. The corpse of the fox fills March with wonder: she passes her hand tremulously down the beautiful, thick, full tail, and marvels over the sharp, penetrating, vicious teeth. The night before Henry, on Banford's insistence, is to leave the farm, March puts on a dress, and the young man is overwhelmed by a sudden, startled awareness of her femininity and her womanly body. He draws her out into the night, and Banford is left sobbing and wailing, her thin shoulders shaking in an agony of grief. Once March has recognised the reality of Henry's passion, she feels at peace and secure with him; and thence feels afraid of Banford. Henry returns to his camp; with absence of his physical being, March regains her equilibrium, and writes to him trying to cry off the marriage—she has returned to Banford, and takes her evaluation of the situation from Banford. So Henry returns and kills Banford, leaving March helpless in grief and agony, but beaten, submissive, no longer resisting him. She knows he has won her. Even so, he has not got her completely. She broods and muses, her eyes dark and vacant; the great effort of manly responsibility is removed from her life, she no longer has to be active, straining to support Banford, to work the farm, to hold their life together. She misses the necessity of exerting herself in action and love: although she feels the desirous necessity of relaxing into Henry's life, letting him take the responsibility, she cannot quite do it. They are going away to Canada. Perhaps over the sea, in a new world, the potentiality of a new life, a new relationship, will grow within her. *The Fox*

MARIA: Daughter of Juana, Kate Leslie's housekeeper; a shy, timid, bird-like thing, with big eyes that seem to absorb the light around her. Both of Juana's daughters trespass on Kate's privacy, Maria with unsolicited physical intimacies—all the more unwelcome since (like her sister) she is a generous patron of lice. *The Plumed Serpent*

MARIA DEL CARMEN: Wife of bricklayer Julio, Juana's cousin. *The Plumed Serpent*

MARRIOTT: A gentleman-farmer from Ambergate, acquaintance of Tom Brangwen. *The Rainbow*

MARSHALL: Married to Lottie Crich, he is an offensive fool. *Women in Love*

MARTIN: A German friend of Countess zu Rassentlow and Baroness von Prelau-Carolath; very erect and military, handsome and clean-shaven; speaking in a quick, precise way; blue eyes strained a little too wide—one can see the war in his face. To Hannele he is representative of their German men-friends, an undeniable, real presence. By comparison Captain Hepburn seems unreal, shadowy, negative; but ultimately the comparison is reversed, and as the Captain begins to dominate her life, people like Martin fade into insignificance. *The Captain's Doll*

MARTIN: Manservant of Don Ramón Carrasco; he is murdered defending his *patrón* during the attempt at assassination. *The Plumed Serpent*

MARUCA: A sewing-girl from Mexico City, with a grudge against Don Ramón. She assists her lover Guillermo to enter his *hacienda* in the unsuccessful attempt to murder her master; she is subsequently executed/sacrificed/murdered by Cipriano on the 'night of Huitzilopochtli'. *The Plumed Serpent*

MÄRZ, FRÄULEIN: Young, slim and pretty, a secretary to Hermione Roddice. *Women in Love*

MASSY, THE REVEREND EDWARD: A young clergyman, an Oxford M.A., descendant of an old Cambridgeshire family, and in possession of private means, who comes to Aldecross as curate during Mr. Lindley's illness. Contrary to the hopeful expectations of the Lindley girls, he is a small, *chétif* man, no bigger than a boy of twelve, bespectacled and extremely timid; but with an inhuman kind of self-assurance. 'What a little abortion!' is Mrs. Lindley's verdict. He is deficient in the full range of human feelings, but has a strong philosophical mind, from which he seems to derive life. Intellectually he has evident powers: physically his being is 'unthinkable'. His conversation is abstract and balanced, without personal conviction or spontaneous exclamation, but only cold, rational assertion. His most annoying habit is a 'sneering little giggle' which accompanies the perception of absurdity or foolishness in another person—he is exquisitely amused by stupidity. But he has no genuine humour, only this inhuman satiric edge: in personal relationships he is never actually there. He remains apart in his own rarefied little world, protecting himself from his own insufficiency. He is a 'perfect Christian' in the recognition and performance of his duties; to the Lindley family he proffers extremes of kindness, but his kindness almost frightens Mary—because it is so impersonal and inhuman, a calculated well-doing. But she submits to him, and they marry. He is scrupulously kind, just and considerate; but cold and self-complete, and out of his weakness comes a cold, domineering will, assertive and blind, like a machine. He becomes obsessed by the idea of his child: his terror is for its safety and well-being—though he has little physical contact with it, doesn't play with it or kiss it, yet it dominates him and empties his mind. The world becomes all baby for him; and in the child he finds an appropriate object for his incessant, inexorable, mechanical solicitude. *The Daughters of the Vicar*

MATILDA, AUNT: *see* Watson, Mrs.

MATTHESON, SIR JOSHUA: A learned, dry baronet of fifty, who is always making witticisms and laughing at them heartily in a harsh horse-laugh. A guest of Hermione Roddice at Breadalby, he is an elderly sociologist, whose mental fibre is so tough as to be insentient; he has a strong mentality, always working, but always *known*—never original, creative, new. *Women in Love*

MAX: A tall German Swiss, with almond eyes and a flattish face, and a rather stiff, ramrod figure; a member of the Natcha-Kee-Tawara travelling theatrical troupe. Usually quiet and unobtrusive, Max can assume an air of *hauteur* and overbearing; and on one such occasion he insults Cicio, in consequence of which the Italian stabs him slightly with a property knife. *The Lost Girl*

MAY, CHARLES: Friend and guest of Sir Clifford Chatterley at Wragby Hall, an Irishman who writes scientifically about stars. He is a believer in 'the life of the mind'; sex should be free and promiscuous, because it is merely a 'sensation', like drinking or dancing—an interchange of sensations instead of ideas. *Lady Chatterley's Lover*

MAY, MR.: With a plump, pink, fat face and light blue eyes, he drifts to Woodhouse looking for a 'managing' job. He has acquired certain American characteristics, such as an ostentatious private innocence—he advertises how seriously he takes his family obligations—combined with a complacent unscrupulousness in 'matters of business'. He is clean-shaven and immaculately smart—but his clothes are old-fashioned, so his rather expensive smartness is detrimental to his image. He manages the cinema for James Houghton, and establishes a sexless intimacy with Alvina, 'like a disconsolate bird pecking up the crumbs of her sympathy'. *The Lost Girl*

MAY, MRS.: Ancient, bent and deaf, she is Frank Beardsall's landlady while he lives, and tends his corpse in death. *The White Peacock*

MAYHEW, MAUD: Sister of the rakish, horsey Mayhew brothers; unhappily married and separated, reserved and silent, she keeps house for her pleasure-loving brothers. *The White Peacock*

MAYHEW, TOM: Acquaintance of George Saxton; a pleasure-loving rake, addicted to whisky, gambling and horses. Cyril is impressed by his 'rather vulgar beauty' and his ineffectual talk. *The White Peacock*

MEE, LOUIS: A friend of Angus and Francis in Florence; a little man whose conversation apparently matches his stature. *Aaron's Rod*

MEG: Later Mrs. Saxton, wife of George. The 'daughter of the Ram Inn', a voluptuous and sensuous physical woman. Cyril has never seen a woman with more physical charm, as she smiles in her fresh, frank way; her cheeks gleam like satin when she laughs, her suave, tawny neck is bare and bewitching. As the mother of George's children, Meg becomes something of a Magna Mater: she handles the children with beautiful gentleness, and is perfect in this pose, drooping her head with a madonna-like grace. George reflects with some perplexity, anger and bitterness, that Meg had found no such pleasure in his passionate physical presence. *The White Peacock*

MELLING, MR.: An old, decaying clerk in the office of Thomas Jordan's Surgical Appliance Factory; wearing a round smoking cap of black velvet embroidered with red and green, he coughs and opens letters. *Sons and Lovers*

MELLORS, BERTHA: The estranged wife of Oliver Mellors. When he married her she was 'common, but with a sort of sensual bloom', and physically desirable. But she treats him with insolence, and gradually their sexual relations become dominated by her greedy and aggressive, exorbitantly demanding female will, which Mellors despises. Eventually she runs off with a collier from Stacks Gate. *Lady Chatterley's Lover*

MELLORS, CONNIE: Mellors' daughter: a self-assured little girl with bold dark eyes; a 'spoilt, false little female'. *Lady Chatterley's Lover*

MELLORS, OLIVER: Sir Clifford Chatterley's gamekeeper; a man of the old style, moderately tall and lean, with red face and moustache and distant eyes; with curious, swift yet soft movements. He is like a gentleman, but a quick, separate fellow, alone but sure of himself. In his solitary aloneness, he is like an animal, brooding, recoiling from human contact. When Connie encounters him, it is the man's solitary singleness, his stillness and his timeless sort of patience, that touch her. He at first is oppressed by her presence, feeling that she is trespassing on his privacy: he has reached a point where all he wants in life is to be left alone. He especially wants to avoid coming again into contact with a woman: 'his last refuge was this wood; to hide himself there'. But his isolated reserve and privacy are broken by the irresistible appeal of the forlorn and unhappy Constance; and he realises that isolation is not possible. As Connie's lover he reawakens her to a new world of human touch and contact, of vital relationship with the living and growing things in the wood. As a

84

man he believes above all else in 'warm-heartedness in love', and in men having 'the courage of their own tenderness'. And in the face of a hostile and destructive world, he believes in his love for Connie; there rests his commitment and his faith: 'I believe in the little flame between us; for me now, it's the only thing in the world.' *Lady Chatterley's Lover*

MICHAELIS (MICK): A young Irishman who has made a fortune by his plays in America; he is 'the last word in what is caddish and bounderish, a hopeless outsider'. But Clifford invites him to Wragby and applauds his success, despite his misgivings about the man's lack of breeding. But when he turns his slow, full eyes, drowned in fathomless disillusion, on Connie, he seems to her 'so old—endlessly old—an outcast, but with the desperate bravery of his rat-like existence'. As Connie's lover he is curiously child-like, tender and defenceless; he rouses in her a wild compassion and yearning, and a wild, craving physical desire, which he is unable to satisfy. In a way she loves him. But he is hopeless, and she cannot love in hopelessness. And he, 'being hopeless, couldn't ever quite love at all.' *Lady Chatterley's Lover*

MILLICENT: Lady Daphne Apsley's maid. *The Ladybird*

MIRABAL: A young man, guest of Don Ramón Carrasco at Tlalpam, lean and pale, and burning with an intense, crazy energy. He is an intellectual devotee of Quetzalcoatl, and a small-time prophet of the coming of the old gods to Mexico. *The Plumed Serpent*

MITCHELL, DR.: An energetic man, quite rich and a bachelor, about fifty-four years old; tall, largely-built, with a good figure, a red, clean-shaven face, and blue eyes. He laughs and talks rather mouthingly, and is pompous and overbearing with his patients. He is lordly and condescending to Alvina Houghton, who tolerates him as a *poseur*; though he *seems* distinguished, and there is a certain graceful, boyish attractiveness about him. He makes up his mind to marry her, and dreams of the luxurious pleasures of their life together. As a commercial proposition and a domestic opportunity the offer appeals to Alvina; and the man himself is 'quite presentable'. They become engaged; but before very long Alvina rebels against this compromise with comfort and complacency, and departs. *The Lost Girl*

MITCHKA (BARONESS ANNAMARIA VON PRIELAU-CAROLATH): A handsome woman with a warm, dark-golden skin and clear black eyebrows over her russet-brown eyes; her manner is usually a kind of roguish coyness. The friend and partner of Hannele, she is mistakenly assumed to be Captain Hepburn's lover by his inquisitive wife. Later when Alexander tries to seek out the two refugees, he discovers that Mitchka is dead—shot in a riot in Salzburg, possibly by a lover. *The Captain's Doll*

MONSELL, MR.: An American friend of Richard Lovat Somers, who stays with him in Cornwall. *Kangaroo*

MONTES, SOCRATES TOMÁS: President of the Mexican Republic—referred to ironically as 'el Jesús Cristo de Mexico'. He later assists Don Ramón in establishing the worship of Quetzalcoatl. *The Plumed Serpent*

MOREL, ANNIE: Sister of Paul; as a child she is a tomboy and a 'flybie-skybie'; 'intensely fond' of Paul. Later she becomes a teacher; and joins forces with Mrs. Morel in disapproving of Miriam. Marries Leonard. *Sons and Lovers*

MOREL, ARTHUR: As a child, Arthur is his father's favourite; he listens enthralled to Walter's stories of life down the pit. He is a quick, careless, impulsive boy, a good deal like his father. In appearance he is 'the flower of his family', graceful and full of life, with his dark brown hair and fresh colouring, and his dark blue eyes. He has a generous manner, but an uncertain, fiery temper, and is selfish, wild and restless, thoughtless and hotheaded. In a moment of rashness he enlists in the army: later he reappears, resplendent and handsome in uniform, but still restless, with something gnawing at him—he is never still. He marries a pregnant Beatrice Wyld, and initially chafes and frets at restrictions; but then the Coppard grit comes out in him—he buckles to his work, undertakes his responsibilities, acknowledges that he belongs to his wife and child, and makes a good best of it. *Sons and Lovers*

MOREL, GERTRUDE: Born in Nottingham, the daughter of a

good old burgher family, famous Independents who became stout Congregationalists; she has clear blue eyes and a broad brow, a rather small woman of delicate mould, but resolute bearing. She has a receptive mind, loving ideas, and is considered very intellectual; 'she liked most of all an argument of philosophy or religion with some educated man.' So when the proud and romantic Gertrude marries a collier, she sees herself as coming down in the world, to what she considers a state of 'dreary endurance'—the struggle with poverty and ugliness and meanness. In her relationship with her husband, Walter, she is resolute and inflexible: she cannot be content with the man as he is, but insists that he should become what she wants him to be—so that, in seeking to make him nobler, she destroys him. Gradually she casts him off, and turns for love and life to the children. After William's death, she relapses into mute despair, but Paul's illness draws her back to life, and the two 'knit together' their lives into perfect intimacy. Her life now roots itself in Paul. She has a great belief in his powers and talents; through Paul, life for her seems rich in promise; in Paul, she is to see herself fulfilled, her struggle vindicated. 'Wherever Paul went, she felt her soul went with him. Whatever he did, she felt her soul stood by him.' *Sons and Lovers*

MOREL, MRS. (SENIOR): Walter Morel's mother; a bitingly sharp-tongued and sharp-practising woman who overcharges her son on the rent, is stingingly contemptuous of his wife's ladylike airs. *Sons and Lovers*

MOREL, PAUL: Son of Gertrude and Walter. Like his mother, he is slight and rather small; a pale, quiet child, with grey eyes that seem to listen, and a full, drooping underlip. As Paul grows older, and particularly after the death of William, he grows closer to his mother—they 'share lives'; everything he does is for her. His primary interest is his painting, which is stimulated by his mother, and from his boyhood sweetheart Miriam Leivers he draws the same fertilising influence: from his contact with Miriam he gains 'insight', while from his mother he derives a life-warmth, and the strength to create. Miriam is able to kindle his imagination, to urge the life-warmth into intensity, like a white light. As the intimacy with Miriam develops into adolescent love, Paul finds that the intimacy has been kept so abstract, so much a matter of soul, of thought and consciousness, that it remains a platonic friendship—with Miriam he is always on 'a high plane of abstraction, when his natural fire of love is transmitted into a fine stream of thought.' The idea of sexual contact between them is for both of them suppressed into a shame; and Paul is almost too shrinking and sensitive to kiss her. Eventually Paul breaks off with Miriam: his accusation against her is that she does not want to *love*—her eternal and abnormal craving is to *be loved*. She is negative, not positive. He abandons Miriam and comes back to his mother. There is one place in the world that stands solid and does not melt into unreality; the pivot and pole of his life, his mother. She supports his life; so naturally her death is to Paul a great gap in life, 'a tear in the veil, through which his life seemed to drift slowly, as if he were drawn towards death.' But Paul does not want to die. 'He would not give in.' *Sons and Lovers*

MOREL, WALTER: A collier, husband of Gertrude, father of William, Annie, Paul and Arthur. As a young man, he is handsome, vigorous and humorous—full of colour and animation. To Gertrude Coppard he has the beauty and glamour of *physical* being, the 'sensuous flow of life'. He can be tender and considerate; and when working, or doing odd jobs round the house, he is at peace, and 'happy in his man's fashion'. But as Mrs. Morel discovers, he is also irresponsible, unable to fulfil his obligations; he deceives her over bills and money, his past and his drinking. The husband and wife are too much opposites: he is purely physical, she is moral and religious; he is purely working-class, she an educated *bourgeoise*. At work he is rebellious and outspoken, and loses the favour of the pit-managers, upon whom a butty depends for the quality of his 'stall'. The conflicts in Walter's marriage and his own nature make him drink heavily; and on several occasions there are quarrels, fights and physical violence in the Morel home. On one such occasion the miner flings a drawer at his wife, and the baby Paul is 'baptised' into hatred of his father by a drop of blood falling from his mother's cut brow. In the 'deadlock of passion' that develops between husband and wife, she is the stronger: Morel becomes withdrawn, shrinking, taking refuge in brutal behaviour; or he escapes into the warm intimacy and comradeship of the public house. Gradually the wife abandons him, casts him off, and becomes exclusively absorbed in the children; her husband is left an empty husk. In later life he becomes confirmed in his 'disgusting' and 'degenerate' ways, becoming mean and despicable, a perpetually ugly irritant to the souls of his family. But traces continue to reappear of his old warmth, his old tenderness, his old humanity; as when he plays with the baby Arthur, who is very much 'his' child; or when the children join him in some job of work, such as making fuses for blasting; or when his wife, collier-fashion, washes his back, and together they shyly recall and recreate the intimacy and affection of their former relationship. *Sons and Lovers*

MOREL, WILLIAM: The eldest Morel child; clever and success-ful, his mother's pride. A careless, yet eager-looking fellow, who walks with long strides, sometimes frowning, often with his cap pushed gaily to the back of his head. He learns shorthand and becomes a clerk; consorts with the 'bour-geoisie of Bestwood'; and gets a situation in London at £120 a year, becoming an accredited 'gentleman'. But William becomes inextricably involved in a futile and destructive relationship with 'Gipsy' (Lily Western): he loves her for her elegance and beauty, but hates her affectations, her silliness, her shallow nature, and the sophisticated ease with which she treats his own family ('the working classes') as servants. He finds her unforgivably deficient in his mother's qualities— intelligence, responsibility, integrity; and he desperately and prophetically insists that 'three months after I am buried, she'll have forgotten me'. Emotional stress and overwork contribute to a serious illness, and Mrs. Morel finds William in London delirious and dying. His death leaves her over-whelmed with emptiness and despair, devoid of 'her old bright interest in life'—until Paul falls ill and threatens to follow his brother. Three months after William's death, 'Gipsy' has forgotten him. *Sons and Lovers*

MOTHER OF THE MAN WHO DIED: She comes to seek him risen near his empty tomb: but he shrinks from connection with anyone. He wants to be intrinsically alone: to let his former existence rest in death. *The Man who Died*

N

NEWTON: A friend of Paul Morel's; a big, jolly fellow, with a touch of the bounder about him, he accompanies Paul on a weekend to Blackpool. *Sons and Lovers*

NORRIS, MRS.: The widow of an English ambassador; an elderly woman, rather like a conquistador herself. She plays the ruthlessly manipulating hostess in her big, ponderous old house in the village of Tlacolula. *The Plumed Serpent*

NUT-NAT (otherwise NAT-NUT): A cripple with inturned feet and no roof to his mouth, who sells nuts in the public houses in Ilkeston; the child Anna Brangwen dislikes him. *The Rainbow*

O

O'BURK TRACY, PADDY: A tall, thin, well set-up man with trembling hands and a face like a beetroot; with light blue eyes twinkling wickedly behind their slight wateriness. Paddy is waiting to marry his son Patrick to Miss Mackinnon, but the wedding is delayed by the premature arrival of the bride's baby—'a foine boy!' *The Boy in the Bush*

OLIVE: Friend of Louisa and Helena Verden, accompanies them to Cornwall. *The Trespasser*

ORDERLY, THE: A youth of about twenty-two, of medium height, and well-built, with strong, heavy limbs, warm and young. His face is sunburnt and swarthy, with a soft, black, young moustache; firmly marked eyebrows stand out over the dark, expressionless eyes, that never seem to think, but only to receive life direct from the senses, unconscious and blind and instinctive. His movements are free and self-contained. His warm physical presence involuntarily imposes itself upon his master the Captain—the officer notices his strong, shapely body, and is moved to flashes of irritation by the blind, instinctive sureness of movement, like some unhampered young animal. The orderly feels constrained by the latent feeling between them and is uneasy: he wants to retain the abstract neutrality of a servant; being forced into a personal relationship makes him feel like a caught wild thing. Under the Captain's taunting and bullying, the orderly keeps himself intact, trying to serve the abstract authority and avoid the man, trying to avoid personal hate—but despite himself the hate grows, responsive to the officer's passion. The orderly finds some relief in the company of his sweetheart: but the Captain, in perverse jealousy, tries to keep them apart. Then in a madness of irritation, and in gratification of deep and violent emotions, the officer brutally assaults the young man, leaving him dulled and sick, slack and nerveless, stupefied and inert. Yet still he must awake, get up, return to the Captain's service, and the intolerable emotional tension and physical proximity. While the Captain seems to gain from the gratification of his feelings in firmness and pride of life, the orderly feels negated and defeated, shadowy and non-existent. He obeys the Captain's commands with mechanical obedience— but within him accumulates a core into which all the energy of his young life is compact and concentrated—there at the centre of his chest is himself, firm, not to be plucked to pieces. Gradually the Captain begins to perceive this integrity and strength of personality, so that he hesitates and slightly retreats; seeing his opportunity, moved to a torment of flaming anger, the orderly murders the officer, feeling pleasure and a passion of relief in the gratification of his hate. Delirious and feverish the soldier wanders aimlessly away, no longer conscious of his physical existence. From the rage of madness and suffering he falls into a dream of anguish; he is broken into fragments, his hunger and thirst seem like sensations separate from himself. He is found dying from heat and hunger and thirst, oblivious and blind. The Captain and his orderly are buried together; one white and slender, rigid in marmoreal repose; the other looking as if every moment he might rouse into life again, so young and unused, from slumber. *The Prussian Officer*

P

PABLO: Military doctor, attends Don Ramón Carrasco when wounded by would-be assassins. *The Plumed Serpent*

PALESTRA, THE CONTESSA: A little Italian countess, guest of Hermione Roddice at Breadalby. She takes notice of everybody, playing her little game, objective and cold, like a weasel watching everything, extracting her own amusement, never giving herself in the slightest. *Women in Love*

PALMER: Gudrun Brangwen's boy-friend, an electrician in the mines, an earnest, clever man, a scientist with a passion for sociology. He is 'really impersonal', having the fineness of an elegant piece of machinery. He is too cold, too destructive to really care for women, too great an egotist. Gudrun and Palmer are in one sense elegants; in another sense two units, adhering to the people, teeming with the lives of the distorted colliers. *Women in Love*

PANCRAZIO: Cicio's uncle, a smallish, rather battered-looking shabby Italian of sixty or more, with a big moustache and reddish rimmed eyes, and a deeply-lined thin face. He is impassive and abstract as a Red Indian. Alvina and Cicio live in his house in Italy. *The Lost Girl*

PAPPLEWORTH, MR.: A thin, sallow man with a red nose, quick, staccato, and smartly but stiffly dressed. There is something rather 'doggy' about him, rather smart, and rather 'cute and shrewd', and something warm, and something slightly contemptible about him. He works at Thomas Jordan's Surgical Appliance Factory and is Paul Morel's immediate boss. *Sons and Lovers*

PARROT, THE: A farm labourer on George Saxton's farm, with a hooked nose, a pale fleshy face, and dull-sighted eyes. He had been a very large man, but is now grey and bending at the shoulders. He tells brutal stories in a slow, laconic fashion, to which George listens with perverse, uncanny relish. *The White Peacock*

PEARSE, MILLICENT MAUD: *see* Skrebensky, Baroness

PEASANT: A poor peasant living in a little mud-brick cottage near Jerusalem, with a dirty little inner courtyard, a fig tree, a few scruffy chickens and a dull donkey. He works hard among the vines and olives and wheat of his master, and then returns to sleep in his mud-hut. But he is proud of his young cockerel: resplendent in black and orange feathers, with a proud, arched neck, and a shrill, defiant crow. When the peasant meets the man who has died, his quick shifty eyes quail, and he is powerless under the look of deathly indifference and strange, cold resoluteness. Hesitating and unwilling, he allows the man to hide and rest in his house. To the man who died the peasant represents the littleness, the grasping covetousness, the natural inertia of the people of the 'little life', the 'little day', which he wants to transcend. *The Man who Died*

PEASANT'S WIFE: A black-browed, youngish woman who doesn't work too hard; throwing a little grain to the hens, or cutting green stuff with a sickle for the dull donkey. She feeds and looks after the man who has died, trying to rouse him: she wants him to desire her. And though he feels the appeal of her soft, crouching, humble body, he cannot desire her. He cannot mingle with her thoughts, her consciousness; her little soul is hard, and short-sighted, grasping, her body has its own little greed, and no true reverence for the return gift. *The Man who Died*

PEDRO: Elder son of Don Ramón Carrasco. He is more disposed to love his father than his younger brother Cyprian; but both children have been set against him by their religion, their education, and their mother. *The Plumed Serpent*

PHILLIPS, BILLY: see Pillins, Billy

PHILLIPS, BILLY (BILLY PILLINS): A childhood friend of the Brangwen sisters Ursula and Gudrun. With his brothers Clem and Walter he lugs the hair and rips the pinafores of the 'superior' Brangwen girls. *The Rainbow*

PHILOSOPHER: When the Priestess of Isis is a young girl in Rome, she asks an aged philosopher if all women are born to be given to men? His answer is that certain rare women are not inspired to open and blossom by ordinary men: they wait for the re-born man; just as the lotus does not respond to the sun, but opens to a dark, unseen sun that shines in the darkness of night. She will be a lotus, and will wait for the unborn man. *The Man who Died*

PHOENIX (GERÓNIMO TRUJILLO): Servant to Mrs. Witt and afterwards to Lou Carrington: an American half-breed, son of a Mexican father and a Navajo Indian mother. He has straight black hair, a thin black moustache, and rather curiously-set dark eyes; long cheeks, and a slouching, diffident, sardonic bearing. 'In the golden suavity of his high-boned Indian face, there was a blank, lost look that was almost touching. But in the smallish dark pupils of his eyes, the dagger-point of light still gleamed—an unforgettable glint of the Indian.' In England, Phoenix's consciousness tends to inhabit the phantasm-world of remembered Arizona, or a phantasmagoric, prehistoric twilight where St. Mawr looms undaunted and unsurpassed. But on returning to America he adopts a more social role, that of the gigolo prepared to sell himself to his mistress for all the thrills and excitements of the white man's world, motor cars and moving pictures and ice-cream soda. He loses in Lou's eyes his mystery: she has already gone beyond Phoenix into a deeper communion, and thenceforth needs him only as a servant. *St. Mawr*

PILLINS, BILLY: Childhood friend of the Morel children. *Sons and Lovers*

PINK-EYE PERCY: A 'superior young Queenslander' who had been sent west because his father found him unmanageable: not a bad sort. He marries Monica Ellis, pregnant with Red Easu's child. *The Boy in the Bush*

PINNEGAR, MISS: Manageress of the work-girls in James Houghton's shop: rather short, stout, mouse-coloured, creepy, with pale grey eyes and a padding step, a soft voice, and purple cheeks. She achieves an insinuating ascendancy over James Houghton with her quiet, triumphant assurance. While James indulges in his airy and disastrous commercial fantasies, Miss Pinnegar provides a solid financial base by grinding out strong, serviceable shirts and aprons for the colliers and their wives. Miss Pinnegar lives to uphold the high-minded dignity of Manchester House after James Houghton and Miss Frost have departed; and it is she who delivers to Alvina the ultimate reproach of Woodhouse morality: 'you're a lost girl!' *The Lost Girl*

POLDI, HERR REGIERUNGSRAT VON: Local governor of a district in the Bavarian Tyrol, and fiancé to Hannele. He is not at first sight prepossessing: approaching fifty, he is stout and rather loose; and in his flapping full-bottomed coat, he looks lower-middle-class. But in fact, while by political necessity he is a republican, by nature he is a monarchist and an imperialist, a true Austrian. He is really much finer and subtler than he looks; once you become accustomed to his fat face, with its fine nose and slightly bitter, pursed mouth, he resembles the busts of some of the late Roman emperors. And there is something grand about him, despite his baggy bourgeois appearance; something sweeping and careless about his soul; big, assertive, without littleness, meanness or coarseness. And most attractive is his talk, witty and voluble and versatile; with a subtle stoicism, an unsentimental epicureanism, a reckless hopelessness. To Hannele he seems almost boyish and impulsive, but also eternal; she is deeply impressed by the careless indifference and the *grande geste* of his old imperialist manners. He makes her feel like a queen in exile. Still, when Captain Hepburn turns up from nowhere, for Hannele Herr von Poldi begins to fade into insignificance. *The Captain's Doll*

POLLY: Overseer of the spiral machinists at Thomas Jordan's Surgical Appliance Factory: a small woman with a red serge blouse, her black hair done on top of her head. A 'proud little bantam', she is very kind to Paul Morel. *Sons and Lovers*

PRENDY, FATHER: Mission priest in the Australian town of Paddy's Crossing; Jack Grant and Tom Ellis find him waiting to marry a heavily pregnant Miss Mackinnon to Patrick O'Burk. *The Boy in the Bush*

PRESCOTT, MR.: Grandfather to Mary Henrietta Urquhart, the Princess. The little girl fascinates the old man; he is spellbound, and in a way in love with her. He broods and

95

muses over her in her absence, craving to see her again. He cherishes the fond hope that she might come to live with him, if her father will give her up. Mr. Prescott dies when the Princess is nineteen, leaving her a considerable fortune. *The Princess*

PRESCOTT, HANNAH: *see* Urquhart, Hannah

PRIELAU-CAROLATH, BARONESS ANNAMARIA VON: *see* Mitchka

PRIESTESS OF ISIS, THE: The Priestess serves 'Isis in Search', the goddess who seeks the lost Osiris, and will integrate his fragmentary being into the wholeness and unity of life. She is beautiful, with a face long and pale, dusky blonde hair held under a thin gold net, ivory feet beautiful beneath her white tunic. Above her saffron mantle her dusky-blonde head is bent with endless musings; a woman entangled in her own dream. The man who died is to her the lost Osiris, and she is to heal him and restore him with the touch of her body. But her mother, who looks after her practical affairs, managing the estate and the slaves, is determined to interfere in their union. The man has to depart, but not before he has given a child to the Priestess: great with child by Osiris, her desire and her destiny are fulfilled. *The Man who Died*

PRINCESS, THE: *see* Urquhart, Mary Henrietta

PSANEK, COUNT JOHANN DIONYS: A Bohemian serving as an officer in the German Army, and lying war-wounded in an English hospital; a small man with a black beard, low-browed, with black hair growing low on his brow, thick dark eyelashes, and black eyes. He has a queer, dark, aboriginal face, a small and somewhat translucent nose. There is a touch of mockery about him, intensified by his small, energetic stature, with its fine lines fired by a keen, male energy. But he lies in hospital in England, weary and sick with pain, wishing only to die, to be buried deep beyond memory and suffering, the dark earth heavy above— until visited by the tender ministrations of Lady Beveridge, and the subsequent arrival of Lady Daphne. His bonds with the world of humanity have been broken, leaving him a separate, isolated fragment, until Lady Daphne helps him reawaken to life. He sees in the submerged recklessness of her nature something answering to his own 'outlaw' nature—just as wild animals, foxes, bears, and adders, need a corresponding wildness in their mates. But still he remains reserved and withdrawn, aloof from touch, haughty as a proud little beast looking out from the shadow of its lair. As he talks to Daphne of their spiritual affinity and kinship, a strange thrill of secrecy develops between them; they go beyond sadness and beyond love, into a secret, thrilling communion. Dionys has ceased to believe in love—to him all the love has been used up, and only anger remains. His philosophy is a form of secret knowledge, initiated by ancient rituals, that the real substance of the world is spiritual, a 'dark fire' underlying all matter; that the world of light is an inversion of the true essence of things. In the same way he believes that the 'white' ideology of love and goodness and charity is spurious and unreal compared with real love, which is wild as a wild-cat in the darkness. He is convinced that Lady Daphne, although she inhabits the secondary, 'white' world in her rational consciousness, is in truth a wild-cat in the darkness. Responding to statements of Major Basil's philosophy of love and goodness, Dionys offers the alternative religion of the 'blessed god of destruction'—a man's god, with a hammer of destruction to batter down the falseness and corruption of the man-made world. His values are 'obedience, submission, faith, belief, responsibility, power'. He expects personal submission from other men, not from his position as a hereditary aristocrat, but from his nature as a *natural* aristocrat: a man whose soul is alone, able to be alone, to choose and command. When Daphne offers herself to him as a lover, he feels that though he has no future in the life of his day, he is one of the lords of the after-life—either as one of those whose spiritual power will inherit the earth, or as one of the lords of the un-dead. He has no power in the day, or in the world of the day: but in the night and the darkness, Daphne is his nocturnal bride. *The Ladybird*

PURDY, JERRY: Walter Morel's pal: a foxy-faced man, cold and shrewd, callously indifferent to his consumptive wife and his neglected children. *Sons and Lovers*

R

RACKETT, DR.: An inmate of the Ellis household at Wandoo, the educator of Lennie Ellis: he is beginning to lose his Oxford drawl and take on some of the Australian ding-dong. But he will never be colonial, if he lives in Australia for a hundred years. A secret opium-eater. *The Boy in the Bush*

RADFORD, MRS.: Clara Dawes' mother: about sixty, stately, almost martial, with a severe face, she sits entombed in a mountain of drawn lace. There is something determined about her: though her face is falling loose, she has the strength and *sang-froid* of a woman in the prime of life. *Sons and Lovers*

RASSENTLOW, COUNTESS JOHANNA ZU: *see* Hannele

RATH, MARY: Niece of Mr. George, who lives with Aunt Matilda, his sister: she is dark-faced, humble but assured, darkly confident, with a queer complacency of her own. She is comfortable to talk to, soft and stimulating. She has a certain magnetic heaviness, and a certain stubborn, almost ugly kind of beauty, which is 'like a bitter flower, rising from a very deep root.' She belongs almost entirely to the social world, and there is an element of conventionality and slight smugness in her; but also a 'wild tang'. Jack wants Mary for his second wife after Monica, but out of conventionality Mary indignantly refuses. *The Boy in the Bush*

REBECCA: The Beardsalls' maid. *The White Peacock*

REDBURN, MRS. HATTIE: A staunch little soul, who assists the Somers during their wartime persecution. *Kangaroo*

REID, HILDA: Sister of Constance Chatterley; a woman, though seeming soft and still, of the old Amazon sort, not made to fit with men. She goes on the war-path with Clifford when Connie is ill, and with Connie when she learns of her affair with Mellors. *Lady Chatterley's Lover*

REID, SIR MALCOLM: The once well-known R.A., father of Constance and Hilda. He is moderately stout, with good-humoured selfishness, a dogged sort of independence, and an unrepentant sensuality. He is initially shocked when he hears of Connie's affair with the gamekeeper, but he takes to Mellors, and establishes with him 'the old freemasonry of male sensuality'. *Lady Chatterley's Lover*

RENSHAW, TOM: Fiancé and later husband of Emily Saxton; a well-built, fair man, smoothly and delicately tanned. There is something soldierly, something self-conscious, and something rather preposterous in his bearing. He has a brother, Arthur. *The White Peacock*

RHYS, OWEN: American poet and socialist, cousin and companion to Kate Leslie. Naturally sensitive and kind, he suffers from a peculiarly American despair—'the despair of having missed something'. If anything is a show, he has to see it; and that is what he calls Life. At the bullfight he gorges on sensations which Kate finds intolerably revolting. He later tries feebly to defend Mexican socialism against the universal scepticism and hatred of the national and colonial bourgeoisie. He is dismissed to the U.S. in Chapter IV. *The Plumed Serpent*

RICE, ALEC: A young man whom Jack Grant overhears proposing to Grace Ellis in 'real earnest', and in a low, urgent voice that sounds like a conspiracy. *The Boy in the Bush*

RICO (SIR HENRY CARRINGTON): An Australian, son of a government official in Melbourne, who had been made a baronet. After floating around Europe on a small allowance, 'being an artist', he becomes 'dutifully married' to Lou Witt. He remains a fashionable portrait painter—at least *he* is fashionable, even if his portraits aren't. He is handsome and elegant, though with a certain Bohemian scruffiness, carefully contrived; he behaves in a floridly elegant manner, and yet is as canny and shrewd as any young *poseur* could be. Rico is afraid of life: terrified of his own potentiality for destructive rage and anger, permanently 'quivering with a sort of cold, dangerous mistrust, which he covered with anxious love'. Above all, he is afraid of St. Mawr. He admires the stallion with an artist's detached vision, but fears the life in him. Rico's tense, anxious, irritable gripping on to life culminates in the accident where St. Mawr, spontaneously recoiling from a dead snake, is brutally forced backwards to collapse on to his rider. Injured and full of resentful rage, Rico is determined to have St. Mawr killed, or at best gelded. But his intentions are foiled by his wife's escape: and Rico drifts into the role of wounded hero, graciously receiving the tenderly solicitous ministrations of the florid Flora Manby. *St. Mawr*

RIDLEY, THE HONOURABLE LAURA: A friend of Lou Carrington, with a fresh complexion, hesitant manner, round, startled brown eyes and bobbed hair; she is slightly condescending, slightly impertinent, slightly flirtatious. *St. Mawr*

ROCHARD, MADAME: A plump, pale woman with dark bright eyes and finely-drawn eyebrows: neatly dressed, with grey threads in her black hair. A brilliant dancing *artiste*, she is the leader and matriarch of the Natcha-Kee-Tawara travelling theatrical troupe. *The Lost Girl*

RODDICE, ALEXANDER: The brother of Hermoine, a Member of Parliament; he enters Breadalby, their country estate, striding 'like a Meredith hero who remembers Disraeli', dispensing cordial, easy offhand hospitality. *Women in Love*

RODDICE, HERMIONE: A rich woman, impressive yet repulsive: she carries her long, blanched face lifted up in the Rossetti fashion, seeming almost drugged, 'as if a strange mass of thoughts coiled in the darkness within her, and was never allowed to escape.' She is full of intellectuality and nerve-worn with consciousness; passionately interested in reform, her soul is given up to the public cause. She is eminent in society, in public action; even in the artistic field, she stands equal with the foremost. Her desire is to be invulnerable, impervious, so that no one could put her down. And yet she is vulnerable, tortured, exposed; she craves for something to fill the terrible gap of insufficiency—she craves for Rupert Birkin. But when Hermione expresses her belief in spontaneity, in the life of the instincts, Birkin accuses her of wanting animalism in the head, of deriving a mental thrill from contemplating animal functions with the intellectual consciousness. 'Your passion is a lie—it's your *will*; because you have no dark, sensual body of life.' With Birkin she lives a relationship of pure will; there is an obsession in her to know everything he knows. And her soul writhes in a black subjugation to him because he does not submit to her—he has the power to exist beyond her, despite her. She hates him with a despair that shatters and breaks her down, in ghastly dissolution. Driven to madness by her failure to grasp and hold Birkin, she tries to kill him, violent waves of hatred and loathing breaking in on her mind. He obstructs her life, so she must smash him, in a voluptuous consummation of her ecstasy of hate. But Birkin is not to be killed. 'I don't let you. It is not I who will die.' *Women in Love*

ROLLINGS, MRS.: A widow, acquaintance of the Houghtons, who attends Madame Rochard in her illness. *The Lost Girl*

ROMERO, DOMINGO: A guide at the Rancho del Cerro Gordo, rented by the Princess; a descendant of the Spanish family that had formerly owned the ranch. Domingo had sold it to white people, the Wilkiesons, spent his $2,000, and now works for the white owners as a guide. He is about thirty years old, a tall, silent fellow, with a heavy closed mouth and black eyes, rather sullen. From behind he is handsome, with a strong, natural body, dark and well-shaped, strong with life; but his face is dark, long and heavy, almost sinister, heavy with meaninglessness. But at the centre of his hopelessness is a spark of pride, or self-confidence, or dauntlessness—a spark in the midst of the blackness of static despair. This gives him a certain alert sensitiveness, a certain beauty in his bearing, a certain quickness of intelligence. When the Princess wants to travel up into the Rockies, Romero accompanies her as guide; and in the thick darkness of the primitive forest night she calls to him, appeals to him, to warm her. He feels a great joy and pride surging in him because he has possessed her: he exults in his power over her. His tender luxuriousness and pride make her feel like a victim. She insists that they return immediately, wounding his male pride with her frigid self-sufficiency. But he determines to keep her as a possession—he will *make* her like it, make her want him. He takes her only clothes and flings them into the pool. He finds he cannot conquer her by force of will, however much he violates her; her spirit is hard and flawless as a diamond. But he can shatter her. In a sombre, violent excess he tries to expend his desire for her. Finally her will breaks, and she lapses into hysterical, helpless tears: and afterwards she doesn't care what happens to her. She will marry him, if he wants. But in him the desire is dead; he goes about in a deathly silence, a sheer negation of life; his desire heavy and dead as ice within him. He is ready for death: and he is shot by a search-party. He is remembered by the Princess only as a man who went out of his mind and shot her horse from under her. *The Princess*

ROSEN, WALTER: A deaf Jewish friend of Francis and Angus, who hears nothing of the conversation. *Aaron's Rod*

RUSSELL, DOROTHY: A College friend of Ursula Brangwen, the daughter of a south-country advocate; she spends her spare moments slaving for the Women's Social and Political Union. Queer and intense, with an ivory face and dark hair. She seems very old, and relentless towards herself; yet she is only twenty-two. *The Rainbow*

S

SAINTSBURY, MR.: A horsey, elderly man, rather like an old maid, who loves the sound of titles; owner of the Mews where the Carringtons stable their horses. *St. Mawr*

SAXTON, DAVID: Younger son of the Saxton family. *The White Peacock*

SAXTON, EMILY: Sister of George, Mollie and David, girl-friend of Cyril Beardsall, eventually marries Tom Renshaw. A girl with bright brown eyes, and soft, short black hair, tumbled into loose, light curls. To Cyril she is like Burne-Jones's damsels, with troublesome shadows always crowding across her eyes. 'Some people, instead of bringing with them clouds of glory, trail clouds of sorrow; to them, sorrow is beauty and the supreme blessedness. Emily has the gift of sorrow.' She has an extravagant emotional nature, she quivers with feeling; she has not a strong intellect, nor a heart of light humour; her nature is brooding and defenceless; she knows herself powerless in the tumult of her feelings, and adds to her misfortunes a profound mistrust of herself. *The White Peacock*

SAXTON, GEORGE: A labourer on his father's farm: strong as

a bull, and physically beautiful. Cyril admires the 'noble, white fruitfulness of his form'. But he is uneducated, 'brutal,' socially and intellectually unequal to the girl he loves, Lettie Beardsall. Abandoned by Lettie, he marries the sensuous and voluptuous Meg. But without Lettie, George's centre cannot hold: he drifts through love and marriage, through socialism, into alcoholism, and moral collapse, and physical decay. We leave him dying: 'like a falling tree, going soft and pale and rotten, clammy with small fungi; while the dim afternoon drifted with a flow of thick, sweet sunshine past him, not touching him.' *The White Peacock*

SAXTON, MOLLIE: George's younger sister; talkative and cheeky, educated into sensitivity and irritation at the coarser manners of her brother. *The White Peacock*

SAXTON, MR.: Father of George, Emily, Mollie, David; a big, burly farmer with a half-bald head sprinkled with crisp little curls. *The White Peacock*

SAXTON, MRS: A quaint little woman with big brown eyes, who keeps her soul in a saucepan. *The White Peacock*

SAYWELL, ARTHUR: Rector of Papplewick, father of Yvette and Lucille, son to the intolerable, monolithic Granny. His wife had left him, and he had displayed an intense and not very dignified grief. His hair is almost white, he has a wild-eyed, tragic look—yet somewhere there is a false note: there is 'a certain furtive self-righteousness about him'. When Yvette's intimacy with the unmarried Eastwoods meets with her father's moral disapproval and withering scorn, she realises that however unconventional he may seem in his would-be humorous fashion, at heart he fears any departure from convention: so Yvette is assailed with pious threats and allegations of criminal lunacy. The rector is unable to cope with life, because essentially he has no belief—no 'core of warm belief, no pride of life'. *The Virgin and the Gipsy*

SAYWELL, MRS. ARTHUR (CYNTHIA): The rector's wife, who 'went off' with a young and penniless man, trailing clouds of scandal as she went. Her memory is preserved by her husband and his mother as a disreputable example, and the daughters are occasionally reproached by Granny for their blood-kinship with a fallen woman. The children remember her as 'a great glow, a flow of life, like a swift and dangerous sun in the house, forever coming and going.' They associate her memory with brightness, but also with danger. *The Virgin and the Gipsy*

SAYWELL, CISSIE: Aunt Cissie, sister to the Reverend Arthur, and slave to the reverend Granny; over forty, pale, pious and gnawed by an inward worm, her life has been sacrificed to her mother. The convention of Aunt Cissie's sacrifice is accepted by everyone, including Aunt Cissie, who prays a good deal about it. She has lost her life and her sex, and now, creeping towards fifty, strange great flares of rage come up in her. When Yvette thoughtlessly misappropriates money from Aunt Cissie's precious 'Window Fund', her frustrated rage breaks like a bursting tumour, and Yvette is lashed with extraordinary, impersonal hatred. *The Virgin and the Gipsy*

SAYWELL, FRED: Brother to the Reverend Arthur, Uncle Fred to Yvette and Lucille; a stingy, grey-faced man of forty, who just lives dingily for himself. *The Virgin and the Gipsy*

SAYWELL, GRANNY: Mother of the Reverend Arthur, she presides over the rectory from her armchair, with her stomach protruding; a sort of 'horrible majesty' in her red, pendulous face, and her peering blind blue eyes. Perfectly complacent, she sits in her ancient obesity, and after meals gets the wind from her stomach, 'pressing her bosom with her hand as she "rifted" in gross physical complacency.' Granny is 'one of those physically vulgar, clever old bodies who get all their own way in life by buttering the weaknesses of their menfolk'; and she holds her son Arthur by his feeblest weakness, his 'skulking self-love'. Granny is perhaps the least lamented casualty of the flood which destroys the rectory. *The Virgin and the Gipsy*

SAYWELL, LUCILLE: Elder sister of Yvette, she is more practical, thoughtful and responsible; she does all the extra troubling, slaves conscientiously at her job in the city, and comes home to have her nerves rubbed to frenzy by Granny's 'horrible persistent acquisitiveness and parasitic agedness'. Lucille is the one who openly rebels against Granny's tyranny when the sisters are accused of hereditary degeneracy: ' "You shut up!" she shouted, in a blast full upon the mottled majesty of the old lady.' *The Virgin and the Gipsy*

SAYWELL, YVETTE: Tall, with a fresh, sensitive face and bobbed hair, and young, manly, deuce-take-it-all manners; too confident in her schoolgirl arrogance, and with some of her mother's 'vague, careless blitheness'. When Yvette meets the gipsy's 'bold yet dishonest eyes', something hard inside her meets his stare. But the surface of her body turns to water. He is stronger than she, in her own kind of strength, her own kind of understanding. In the course of a quarrel about some misappropriated money, Yvette discovers in her father the Rector 'the inferiority of a heart which has no core of warm belief in it, no pride of life'. Faced with this vacuum of belief, and assailed by Aunt Cissie's rage of hatred, Yvette begins to recoil from the family: to feel closer to her mother in the amoral sanctity of her sensitive, clean flesh, which the so-called morality of the Saywells succeeds in defiling; and she dreams of the gipsy, of his big, bold eyes, with the 'naked insinuation of desire'. The thought of the gipsy releases the life of her limbs, and makes her hatred of the rectory coalesce in her heart, giving her a sense of power and potency. In the unleashed force of the terrible flood which destroys the rectory and the monumental Granny, Yvette and the gipsy survive, sustain life by mutual help and comfort, sharing the common warmth of physical nakedness. Awakening alone in the ruined house, Yvette finds her gipsy gone, and grieves for him. But practically she is 'acquiescent in the fact of his disappearance. Her young soul knew the wisdom of it.' *The Virgin and the Gipsy*

SCOTT, CYRIL: A fair, pale, fattish young fellow who is attempting to persuade Julia Cunningham to live with him in Dorset. Between them there is a nervous kind of *amour*, based on soul sympathy and emotional excitement. *Aaron's Rod*

SCHOFIELD, ANTHONY: Brother of Ursula's fellow-teacher Maggie Schofield; a market-gardener, strong and well-made, with brown, sunny eyes, and a brown, handsomely-hewn face. He is like a faun or a satyr in the gleam of his golden-brown eyes. Anthony makes Ursula Brangwen alert and aroused by his sensuous power, she becomes all alive, all senses. He asks her to marry him, but she must refuse: he is an animal, and while the life he offers her is fascinating and attractive, he has no soul. 'She was a traveller on the face of the earth, and he was an isolated creature living in the fulfilment of his own senses.' *The Rainbow*

SCHOFIELD, MAGGIE: Standard Three teacher in Brinsley Street school. Ursula befriends her as she alone manages to remain 'personal' in the hostile and disintegrating atmosphere of the school. *The Rainbow*

SECONDE, HILDA: A svelte, petite girl, exquisitely and delicately pretty; a friend of Leslie Tempest. *The White Peacock*

SHARPE, JAMES: A young Edinburgh man with a moderate income of his own, interested in music; he lives near the Somers in Cornwall. *Kangaroo*

SHERARDY, DOCTOR: A little greenish man, a Hindu with bright, completely black eyes; he participates in the intellectual gatherings in the bar-parlour of the Royal Oak, arguing strongly for human responsibility in political affairs. *Aaron's Rod*

SHORT, JIMMIE: A sort of cousin of Tom Ellis; but when Tom, newly returned from two years in the bush, meets him in Perth, he takes his filthy, hairy and dilapidated cousin for a tramp. *The Boy in the Bush*

SHORT, MRS.: A woman who cleans Rawdon Lilly's cottage. *Aaron's Rod*

SISSON, AARON: A good-looking man, pleasant, a checkweighman in the pit, and Secretary of the Union Lodge. But he abandons his job, his wife and children for the life of an itinerant flautist. After being seduced by Josephine Ford, Aaron falls ill from a failure of life in him—he is 'gloomily withheld, retracting from life'. Rawdon Lilly nurses him back to health, but dismisses him when Aaron refuses to submit to Lilly's authority. Later Aaron revisits his wife, who offers him reproach, tenderness and reconciliation; but he feels a 'horror' of her, is 'repelled': 'she wanted to win his own self-betrayal out of him'. Now for Aaron the illusion of love is gone for ever. Love is a battle for mastery, in which woman has been the victor, and is now challenged again by man—but too late, for woman will never yield. Aaron wants to keep the mastery of his own soul, and resolves never again to deliver himself up to the judgement of a woman. He thanks the universe for the 'blessedness of being alone, of perfect singleness'. With this discovery Aaron finds himself beneath the social identity, quiet and free. He comes under the spell of the Marchesa del Torre, who exercises over him the power of a bare, occult force, something he cannot cope with. After they have become lovers, Aaron is confirmed in his hatred of love: 'I don't want kindness or love ... I want the world to hate me, because I can't bear the thought that it might love me.' And his thoughts turn to Rawdon Lilly, like a fate which he resents but which steadies him. In the bombed café, the world finally explodes for Aaron, and his rod is shattered. Nothing is left for him but the thread of destiny which attaches him to Lilly. If he has to give in, he feels it better to give in to Lilly than to a woman, or an ideal, or a social institution. Lilly argues that such a yielding is natural and true—'a deep, fathomless submission to the heroic soul in a greater man'. And Aaron seems to have no choice but to submit. *Aaron's Rod*

SISSON, LOTTIE: A slim, neat woman with dark hair, the wife of Aaron, who abandons her with her children Marjory and Millicent, leaving her angry, resentful, distraught and alone. Later he returns, half-expecting a wild and emotional reconciliation, filled with a violent conflict of tenderness. She reviles him with accusations, contempt, hatred, threats; then reproaches him, with aggrieved tenderness. But Aaron feels that among all her distress there is a self-dramatisation, 'a luxuriating in the violent emotions of the scene in hand'; beneath the wistful reproach, and sombre accusation, and wifely tenderness, beneath the caresses and the pleading, he feels the iron threat, the dominant power of her female will. When he leaves, Lottie reflects that neither of them would ever yield to the other; and come life or death, *she* would never yield. *Aaron's Rod*

SKREBENSKY, ANTON: Son of Baron Skrebensky, an officer in

the Royal Engineers. A young man with a slender figure and soft brown hair brushed up in the German fashion, straight from the brow; his face irregular, almost ugly, flattish, with a rather thick nose; and greenish eyes, pellucid and clear. He strikes Ursula Brangwen as strangely 'acquiescent in the fact of his own being'; self-possessed and self-assured. As they fall in love their relationship is one of daredevil romanticism, but it contains the seeds of a relationship of wills—'he kissed her, asserting his will over her, and she kissed him back, asserting her deliberate enjoyment of him.' It is a magnificent self-assertion on the part of each of them, rather than a flowing together of lives into communion. Skrebensky is a seriously limited figure, who does not believe in the importance of the individual life: he is a soldier, a citizen, and when called upon will do his duty by the army or the nation. To Ursula he seems unreal, a nothingness: 'Are you anybody really?' The individual to Skrebensky is merely a brick in the social fabric, and the unit has no importance except in so far as it represents the whole, the great scheme of man's elaborate civilisation. Skrebensky therefore cannot love; he can never really want a woman with the whole of him, never worship, can only just physically desire. Gradually he feels himself becoming cold, extinct, dead, without individual life; the whole of his being becomes sterile, a spectre, divorced from life. He fills the vacuum of his existence with mechanical sensations; and out of the hollowness of his being asks Ursula to marry him. But their deadlocked relationship develops to a crisis: in a terrible scene Ursula challenges Anton to a bitter and sterile struggle for sexual consummation, in which the man is defeated. He hastens to run away from Ursula, marrying a former acquaintance and disappearing to India. *The Rainbow*

SKREBENSKY, BARON: A Polish exile, a clergyman in Yorkshire. An aristocrat, he expects homage from the common people but is roughly and cruelly received by the Yorkshire colliers. Later his wife dies and he marries a young English girl of good family, Millicent Maud Pearse. *The Rainbow*

SKREBENSKY, BARONESS: The first Baroness is a tall thin woman of noble Polish family, mad with pride.

After her death Baron Skrebensky marries Millicent Maud Pearse, a little, creamy-skinned thing with red-brown hair and the soft, elusive beauty of a ferret. *The Rainbow*

SLAIGHTER, HILDA: A friend of the Saxtons and Beardsalls. *The White Peacock*

SMITH, TOM: A guest of the Tempests' at a Highclose party. He sits staring scornfully over his spectacles with sharp brown eyes. *The White Peacock*

SNOOK, MISS LUCY: A barmaid in the Palace of Circe in the Australian town of Honeysuckle; Tom Ellis with some consternation finds himself more or less accidentally married to her, and quickly makes good his escape. *The Boy in the Bush*

SOMERS, HARRIET: The wife of Richard Lovat Somers, a real beauty, with a fair, radiant face, a charming bearing, and a wonderful fresh zest for life. She has a real, instinctive mistrust of other people; and in her heart of hearts wants to live alone with Somers. She is furiously resentful of Somers' attempts at 'pure male activity', intimacy with other men and participation in political affairs. In so far as he keeps activity separate from her, the activity is defined as trivial in her eyes: she wants to share, to join in, while he insists that some activities should be womanless. Harriet will not permit him to regard any cause or commitment as higher than their marriage; she insists that whatever his external involvements, inwardly he should maintain the connection with her, maintain the flow between them, and safeguard it carefully. *Kangaroo*

SOMERS, RICHARD LOVAT: A writer of poems and essays with an income of £400 a year. In post-war Europe, he has made up his mind that everything is done for, played out, finished, and he must go to a new country. So the smallish, pale-faced man, with a dark beard, well-dressed and with a quiet self-possession, finds himself in Australia. Despite the pressure from his wife Harriet to keep their relationship isolated and self-sufficient, Richard is always moved to participate in other activity, to seek connection with other men. But when Jack Callcott offers him personal comradeship and participation in the Digger movement, he holds back and cannot give himself—mistrust and reluctance quench the thrill of desire. He is drawn to the Diggers, Kangaroo's para-military fascist organisation, because it seems possible that their dictatorship might lead to a new life-form; and on his first meeting with their leader Kangaroo he is overwhelmed by the 'steady loveliness of the man's warm, wise heart'. But ultimately the Diggers seem to him merely destructive; and he begins to disagree with Kangaroo's universal doctrine of love. Finally he feels that he has nothing to do with them: when he is himself, there is in his soul a quiet stillness, an inward trust. He rejects all abstract ideals, God, Love, Humanity, and with them the political causes which uphold the ideals. He wants to be alone, to turn to the old, dark gods, who have waited so long in the outer dark. 'Let me get back to my own self: a man with his soul alone; and the dark god beyond him.' *Kangaroo*

STAPLES: A boy in Ursula Brangwen's class at Brinsley Street school. *The Rainbow*

STRANGEWAYS, OLIVE: Wife of Jack, guests of the Chatterleys at Wragby Hall. She looks forward to the day when women will be freed from the burden of their natural functions, when babies will be bred in bottles. *Lady Chatterley's Lover*

STRUTHERS: A painter, attached to the Bricknell's Bohemian set in London. *Aaron's Rod*

STRUTHERS, WILLIE: Leader of the Australian Socialist Party: very dark, red-faced and thin, with deep lines in his face, a tight, shut, receding mouth, sunken cheeks and deep, cadaverous eyes. He wants to combine the political and economic objectives of socialism with the furthering of new human relationships between man and man; and he asks Richard Somers to help by editing a newspaper. *Kangaroo*

SWALLOW, MR.: A friend of Mr. George, he is present when Jack Grant arrives in Australia. He has a long, lean ruddy face, a large nose and vague brown eyes. *The Boy in the Bush*

T

TEMPEST, LESLIE: A wealthy young man, smart and elegant, skilled in tennis and other 'ladies' accomplishments'; with a fine, lithe physique, suggestive of much animal vigour; his person attractive, but his face less so. But he has a frank, good-natured expression, and a fine, wholesome laugh. More 'eligible' than George Saxton, Leslie is chosen by Lettie Beardsall: and as they eddy unevenly down the stream of courtship, jostling and drifting together and apart, he is unsatisfied, and strives to bring her closer to him, in submission. Gradually she yields; but after marriage she becomes dominant. Leslie becomes less assertive and self-confident, he does not seek to dominate, is now unobtrusive, with a new reserve, gentleness and grace. To Lettie he is unfailingly attentive, courteous, undemonstrative—the abject slave of the unsatisfied woman. *The White Peacock*

TEMPEST, MARIE: Sister of Leslie Tempest, a 'charming little maid', neat and confident, very conservative, full of proprieties, and gently indulgent. *The White Peacock*

TERESA: The second wife of Don Ramón Carrasco, married shortly after the death of Doña Carlota. She is rather small, pale, with loose black hair, and a quiet bearing suggesting independence and authority. Small and apparently insignificant, Teresa has the female power and the 'fierce reverence' of love to make Don Ramón into a 'big, golden, full glory of a man'. Kate Leslie, the woman of the world, clever and handsome, discovers with some resentment and indignation that the quiet, deep passion of connection with Ramón, and the secret, savage, indomitable pride of her own womanhood, make the little Teresa a greater woman than herself. *The Plumed Serpent*

THOMAS, JOHN: Familiar name for Oliver Mellors' penis; first appears in chapter X, but is not named until chapter XIV. *Lady Chatterley's Lover*

TILLY: Cross-eyed servant woman at the Marsh Farm. *The Rainbow*

TOUSSAINT, JULIO: Guest of Don Ramón Carrasco at Tlalpam; sententious and didactic preacher of fascist theories of racial purity, and of the dubious biological view that heredity is dependent on the spiritual character of the act of coition. *The Plumed Serpent*

TRACY, PADDY O'BURK: *see* O'Burk Tracy, Paddy

TRAHERNE, POPPY: A lady of innumerable petticoats, who can whirl herself into anything you like, from an arum lily in green stockings to a Catherine wheel and a cup-and-saucer; one of the variety 'turns' at James Houghton's cinema. *The Lost Girl*

TRAVERS, LOUIE: Baxter Dawes' mistress; works as a machinist at Thomas Jordan's Surgical Appliance Factory. A handsome, insolent hussie who mocks at Paul Morel, yet flushes if he walks with her. She leaves Baxter for a man who is prepared to marry her. *Sons and Lovers*

TREWHELLA, GLADYS: Daughter of Rose and William James, a little girl with long brown hair. *Kangaroo*

TREWHELLA, ROSE: Wife of William James, a brown-eyed Australian with a decided manner, kindly, but a little suspicious. *Kangaroo*

TREWHELLA, WILLIAM JAMES (JAZ): A young Cornishman, rather stout and short and silent, rather pale, with a humorous look in his light grey eyes and at the corners of his mouth. A coal and wood merchant, he is brother-in-law to Victoria Callcott, friend to Jack. He combines a restless, desirous, craving for something with a secretive, maybe treacherous nature; he is a Digger, but his commitment to the movement is essentially limited—he joins for the 'spree', for the 'fun'. He admits to Somers that his involvement in politics is an evasion of the terrible fear of his own emptiness, and of the emptiness of Australia. *Kangaroo*

TRUJILLO, GERÓNIMO: *see* Phoenix

TUKE, EFFIE: An acquaintance of Alvina Houghton, one of the 'toney intellectual élite' of Lancaster. She is having a child, but feels no physical connection with it whatsoever; she believes that the universe is just 'one big machine, and we are part of it'. Her husband Tommy takes exception to the nauseating emotional Italian music of Cicio's serenade, but this does not prevent them getting drunk to stupefaction together. *The Lost Girl*

TWO MEN: Followers of the man who died, who meet him on the road to Emmaus and do not know him. *The Man who Died*

U

URQUHART, COLIN: Husband of Hannah Prescott, father of Mary Henrietta, the Princess. Colin is just a bit mad; a descendant of an old Scottish family, he claims that the royal blood of Scottish kings flows in his veins; an assertion which seems rather ridiculous, and is a 'sore point' to his relatives. He is a handsome man, with wide-open blue eyes that seem sometimes to be looking at nothing; with soft black hair brushed low on his broad brow; and a very attractive body. He has a most beautiful speaking voice, usually rather quiet, diffident, but sometimes resonant and powerful like bronze. He looks altogether like some old Celtic hero out of the hushed Ossianic past; and he is one of those gentlemen of sufficient but not excessive means who wander vaguely about, never arriving anywhere, never doing anything, but always well received in good society. At forty he marries a wealthy Miss Prescott from New England, who becomes the mother of his baby Mary Henrietta, his little Princess, and shortly afterwards dies. The wealthy relatives of his wife try to claim the child, but he courteously, musically and finally refuses. The Prescotts are never real to him: he is unaware of their existence. He travels the world on his moderate income, taking the baby with him. He advises her as a child, never to take notice of other people: all social intercourse is nothing; the only thing that matters is the essential, real self at the core of every living individual. This 'demon' which exists when everything else has been peeled away, belongs to an older, primitive world, and is indifferent to the actual world around it. He sees the Princess as the last of the royal race of the old people: her demon is royal and proud, and must always ignore the claims of inferior souls. People should be treated politely and with consideration: but she must never forget that she is alone, superior, untouched. When her grandfather dies, leaving her a considerable fortune, father and daughter live a life of wandering freedom, camping in the redwood forests, sleeping under the stars, riding, painting, writing poetry. As the years pass, the daughter remains unchanged, still the same dainty, virgin Princess; but the father ages and becomes more and more queer, estranged, given to fits of violence which horrify his daughter. He dies, leaving her scenting the raw, vast open air, after living all those years in the hot-house atmosphere of her father's madness. *The Princess*

URQUHART, HANNAH: At twenty-two the wealthy Miss Prescott is charmed by Colin Urquhart, fascinated by the man with soft black hair, not yet touched by grey, and the wide, rather vague blue eyes. She lives for three years in the mist and glamour of his presence; and then it breaks her. It is like living with a fascinating spectre: he is ghostly, almost oblivious of everything; always charming, courteous, gracious, but absent, not really there. After the first few months his very beauty and haunting musical quality become almost dreadful to her. He is like a strange, living echo: even his flesh is not like the flesh of an ordinary man. Hannah is not robust, and has no great desire to live; so when her daughter the Princess is two years old, she dies. *The Princess*

URQUHART, MARY HENRIETTA (THE PRINCESS, also DOLLIE): Daughter of Colin and Hannah Urquhart. As a child she is a soft, dainty little thing, with dark gold hair that goes a soft brown, and wide, slightly prominent blue eyes, at once candid and knowing. 'She is always grown up; she never really grows up.' She is always strangely wise, and always childish. From her father she learns the two lessons he teaches her: always to be absolutely reticent, intimate with no one; and always to be naively, benevolently polite. As a small child, something crystallises in her character, making her clear and finished, as impervious as crystal. She is erect and remains dainty, always small in physique, almost like a changeling.

She has beautiful little hands, and a complexion of pure apple-blossom. Her father by his influence frames her into an exquisite picture, from which she never steps. In her education she has an uncanny understanding of things, understanding in a cold light, with all the flush of fire absent. She is so assured, and her flower of maidenhood so scentless. She treats servants and hirelings with a condescension masking total, impersonal contempt; and men are enraged at the blasphemous impertinence of her sterility. The power of her spirit does not extend to these 'low' people, and the implacability of their hatred makes her tremble—so she pays her money and turns away. As she grows older she does not change, but remains the same virgin princess, utterly intact, isolated and self-sufficient. When she is thirty-eight, her father dies, leaving her still unchanged, still a dignified, scentless flower. Her soft brown hair fluffs softly round her apple-blossom face; in her voice, manner and bearing she is exceedingly still, like a flower that has blossomed in a shadowy place. Sardonically, the Princess looks out on to a vulgar, princeless world. Her father's death leaves her relieved, but faced with absolute nothingness. She feels the need to do something—an activity she has always considered as the peculiar prerogative of the 'vulgar'. She considers marriage, not in relation to any particular man, but as an abstract proposition in her own mind. Then her mind turns to travel, and accompanied by her companion Miss Cummins she visits a ranch in New Mexico, on the edge of the mountains. She continues to think of 'marriage', but finds no interest in the young eligible men of her social class. The first man who appears real to her is the Mexican-Spanish guide, Domingo Romero; she catches the spark in his eye, and knows instantly that his 'demon' is a fine demon. She feels from him a subtle insidious male kindliness she has never felt before; a subtle gentleness, as if he sends from his heart a dark beam of succour and sustenance. A vague, unspoken intimacy grows up between them. She cannot conceive of *marriage* to Romero: although she feels that their two 'demons', their essential selves, are perhaps already united in spirit, their two social selves are incompatible. The Princess becomes restless on the ranch: she wants to travel up into the mountains, to see wild animals in their natural environment, to look over the mountains into

their secret heart, to see the animals move about in their wild unconsciousness. When they reach the heart of the mountains, a huge and intricate knot of mountains, empty of life or soul, the Princess is frightened by the inhuman quality of the landscape, the massive, gruesome repellent core of the mountains. She wants to turn back. But Romero guides her on, beyond the civilised world which she has always known, and in which she has always been mistress, quietly in command. At last they reach the cabin in the mountains, a tiny hovel in the forest, pervaded by the strange squalor of the primitive world. She feels the immense cold and shadow of the primitive, forest and mountain world; and seeing a bob-cat watching her across the water, with cold, electric eyes of strange intentness, watching her with cold, animal curiosity, demonish and conscienceless, she feels the dread and repulsiveness of the wild. In the intense cold and thick oblivious darkness of the night, she awakes in a conflict of emotions and desires: she wants warmth, protection, to be taken away from herself; and at the same time she wants to keep herself intact, untouched, letting no one have any power or rights over her. But she asks Romero to warm her; and he comes to her, panting like an animal with desire. She has *willed* it to happen to her, and therefore cannot escape; but her only desire is to go away, to be free of him, to be alone. She insists that they return again immediately, back to the world of people. She must regain possession of herself. Romero is deeply humiliated and insulted by her unyielding self-sufficiency and intactness; he throws her clothes into the water to prevent her escaping. But she is stony and absolute in resistance: 'You can never conquer me!' Yet he *has* possessed some unrealised part of her which she never wanted to realise; so Romero's passion racks her inwardly with a burning heat. If only she could be alone again, cool and intact. She will never love any man. Romero is killed by the men searching for her, and she is taken home slightly crazy, hardly remembering—or willing to forget—the experience; recalling only something about a madman who shot her horse from under her. Later she marries an elderly man, and seems pleased.
The Princess

V

VERDEN, HELENA: A girl of twenty-eight, with a strong, vigorous body and heavy blue eyes. As Siegmund MacNair's lover she belongs to the class of 'dreaming women' with whom passion exhausts itself at the mouth; her desire is accomplished in a kiss. 'With her the dream was always more than the actuality.' Siegmund's dreams are the 'flowers of his blood', hers more 'detached and inhuman'. She wants to sacrifice herself to him or possess him, rather than meet him with equal passion. She is winsome and fanciful, loving fancy more than imagination; she loves the 'trifles and toys, the mystery and magic of things'. But her fanciful enjoyment gives way to guilt (she is a 'moralist, of fervent Wesleyan stock') and a terrifying sense of impending doom: 'Fate, ashen grey and black, like a carrion crow, had her in its shadow.' Overcome by these forebodings, she is most utterly alone in Siegmund's embrace; but she experiences alone a moment of mystic ecstasy before the beauty of the sea and sky, in which she stands still and worships—and 'God's fire settles on her like the Holy Spirit'. Siegmund is excluded from this communion of innocence by his 'bitter wisdom of experience'—he is at the point of farewell, and can see through the surrounding glamour the 'ugly building of his real life'. When Siegmund dies by his own hand, Helena is left alone and desolate: she has neither destination nor direction. 'Siegmund was gone; why had he not taken her with him?' *The Trespasser*

VERDEN, MR. and MRS.: Helena's father is a small, white-bearded man with a gentle voice, and a quiet, reserved manner. In his humble reserve there is a dignity which makes his disapproval difficult for Helena to bear. Her mother Mrs. Verden by contrast assails her daughter on her return with playful, affectionate sallies and repeated, flagrant questionings. *The Trespasser*

VIEDMA, GENERAL (DON CIPRIANO): Kate Leslie's first impression of Cipriano is of a rather ridiculous, over-civilised exterior covering a submerged savagery; 'his education lies like a film of white oil on the black lake of his barbarian consciousness.' His manner is superficially cocky and assured, but underneath 'half-savage, shy and farouche'. General Viedma is commander of the Guadalajara division of the federal armed forces: but by means of his charismatic power over the men and the persuasive mythology of the Quetzalcoatl cult, he enjoys all the convenience of a private army, which he uses to defend and advance the interests of Ramón and Quetzalcoatl. The two men share a passionate religious brotherhood, and Cipriano finds his fulfilment in submission to the soul of the greater man. Cipriano exerts the same demonic power over Kate Leslie, who submits to marriage with him, initially by Quetzalcoatl, then legally. In the course of an intimate and elaborate ritual conducted by Ramón, Cipriano assumes completely the identity of the god Huitzilo-pochtli. After his 'incarnation' is held the ritual of the 'night of Huitzilopochtli', in which Cipriano, resplendent in feathers and war-paint, arbitrarily butchers five people in an elaborate ceremony, something between a public execution, a religious service, and a scene from a slaughterhouse. Having appointed himself to divinity, the man-god offers human blood-sacrifice to his own godhead. *The Plumed Serpent*

VILLIERS, BUD: American companion of Kate Leslie and Owen Rhys. Like Owen, he is a sensation-hunter, but in a more determined and cold-blooded way. At the bullfight he is intense and abstract, getting the sensation; not even involved enough to feel sick, he is getting the thrill, coldly and scientifically. *The Plumed Serpent*

VYNER, DEAN and MRS.: A clergyman, neighbour of the Carringtons' in Shropshire. A big, burly fat man with a pleasant manner. A gentleman, and a man of learning, he looks down on Mrs. Witt just a trifle—as a parvenu, an American—and at the same time has a sincere respect for her as a rich woman. He is *charming* to Lady Carrington, and very gracious to Rico. His wife is an invalid. *St. Mawr*

W

WADE, CORINNA: An elderly, quite well-known, very cultured and very well-connected English authoress. She is charming in her white hair and white woollen dress, charming in her old-fashioned manner; 'as if the world were still safe and stable, like a garden in which delightful culture and choice ideas bloomed safe from wind and weather.' *Aaron's Rod*

WALTON, MR. and MRS.: The parents of Beatrice MacNair, who assist her financially after Siegmund's death. *The Trespasser*

WATSON, MRS. (AUNT MATILDA): Mr. George's sister; a large, stout woman, with reddish hair, silk frocks, gold chains, diamond-ringed hands. *The Boy in the Bush*

WEATHERELL, LEO: An acquaintance of the Saywell girls, a bit common, good-natured and well-off. A comfortable, well-nourished, determined little fellow. Yvette Saywell quite unconsciously attracts Leo, and is astonished by his abruptly proposing to her. *The Virgin and the Gipsy*

WEEDON, MRS.: Fellow-gossip of Mrs. Bolton's. *Lady Chatterley's Lover*

WESSON: A miner, thin, rather frail-looking, with a boyish ingenuousness and a slightly foolish smile, despite his seven children. *Sons and Lovers*

WESTERN, LOUISA LILY DENYS: 'Gipsy', sweetheart and fiancée of William Morel; tall and elegant, with a clear, transparent olive complexion, hair black as jet, and beautiful grey eyes. Handsome and elegant, William's betrothed is totally brainless and silly; she can understand nothing but love-making and chatter. With the Morel family she queens it, condescending and playing the grand lady. A few months after William's tragic death, she writes to his mother: 'At a ball last night: enjoyed myself thoroughly. Had every dance—did not sit one out.' *Sons and Lovers*

WHARMBY, MRS.: Landlady of the New Inn at Bretty. *Sons and Lovers*

WIGGINGTON, MR.: Fat, red-haired landlord of the George Inn at Derby. *The Rainbow*

WILKIESON, MRS.: The capable owner of the Rancho del Cerro Gordo, where the Princess stays. *The Princess*

WILKINSON, MRS.: Charwoman of Cossethay Church, who 'descends like a harpy' on Will Brangwen when Ursula vandalises the church. *The Rainbow*

WILLIAMS, VERNON: A thin, ferret-faced boy in Ursula Brangwen's class at Brinsley Street school. He is a defective, with a cunning intelligence, etiolated and degenerate, an actor skilled in mocking the teacher. In a hideously ugly scene Ursula thrashes him for disobedience, an action which 'violates' both child and teacher. Williams' mother protests to Mr. Harby about her son's 'delicacy' of constitution, and the injustice of beating him. *The Rainbow*

WINTER, LESLIE: Clifford Chatterley's godfather, an elderly gentleman, a wealthy coal-mine owner, an old buck of the King Edward school, rather gallant. *Lady Chatterley's Lover*

WINTERBOTTOM, MR.: Assistant cashier in the mining company of Carston, Waite and Co. He pays out the miners' wages, accompanied by remarks that are not funny, trying to supply the humorous mockery while his chief, the great Mr. Braithwaite, supplies the patriarchal admonitions. *Sons and Lovers*

WINTERSLOW, HARRY: A guest of the Chatterleys' at Wragby Hall; he thinks civilisation should improve on human nature by eliminating the body, leaving the spirit untrammelled and free. *Lady Chatterley's Lover*

WITHAM, ALBERT: Brother of Arthur; formerly a schoolteacher, he has been out to South Africa and accumulated some money, and is now taking a belated degree at Oxford. He is 'quite unattractive', tall and thin and brittle, with a pale, dry flattish face; he gives an impression of flatness rather like a lemon sole. He makes the unwarranted assumption that Alvina accepts him as a follower, and smiles on her with a complacent delight, trying to dominate her in his overbearing way. He is approved by James Houghton and Miss Pinnegar as a suitor—but Alvina decides, to their dismay, that she 'can't stand him'. *The Lost Girl*

WITHAM, ARTHUR: A plumber, sly and slow and uneducated; not bad-looking, a tight fellow with big blue eyes, who aspires to keep his 'h's' in the right place, and would have been a gentleman if he could. He is keen after money, and creeps slyly after his own self-importance and power. Alvina is attracted to him, until in a slight accident Arthur makes use of her, without extending her any human recognition. *The Lost Girl*

WITHAM, LOTTIE: Arthur's wife, a bit of a shrew, with social ambitions and no children. *The Lost Girl*

WITT, LOUISE: *see* Carrington, Lady Louise

WITT, MRS. RACHEL: The mother of Lou Carrington. She looks 'curiously young', but with the youth of an earlier generation. She has heavy-lidded, laconic grey eyes, black tilting eyebrows and a slightly powdered skin. With her 'queer democratic New Orleans conceit' she has a savage contempt for the English society in which she has chosen to live. She shares her daughter's sense of the futility of their lives, and would like to destroy her world—she feels a certain admiration for the destructive violence of St. Mawr. Mrs. Witt knows that her nature is a destructive force, but justifies herself by seeking for something indestructible to stand against. 'She wanted to be defeated; and no one had ever defeated her.' When St. Mawr's life and virility are threatened, she performs her only decisive action, escaping to America with the horse and her daughter. In Lewis the groom she glimpses something of the world 'beyond', which is visible to her daughter in St. Mawr. Perhaps behind this little man there lies the great Mystery? But her onslaught on Lewis's chastity meets with a high-principled and determined rejection. In America she lapses finally into an apathy of inactivity, of neutrality, of stony, blank indifference to life. Undefeated, she remains for ever unsatisfied. *St. Mawr*

WOOKEY, GEOFFREY: A heavy, hulking fellow, a year older than his brother Maurice. His blue eyes are unsteady, glancing away quickly, his mouth is morbidly sensitive; his inflamed self-consciousness is a disease in him, making his whole body wince with shame and embarrassment. He has been attracted to Paula Jablonowsky, and she seems attracted to him; but his younger brother has bested him and claimed her in physical passion—and now she prefers Maurice. As Maurice taunts him, Geoffrey's heart swells within him, and the land-scape grows dark before his eyes. He is deeply mortified by Maurice's success; and he feels the danger of sinking into a morbid state from sheer lack of living, lack of interest. As the two brothers are working together on the haystack, the rivalry between them erupts into open physical conflict, and they set themselves against each other like two bulls. Geoffrey, leaning all his weight in resistance against his brother, pushes Maurice off the stack. He almost hopes Maurice is dead: even that seems preferable to the discovery that he is responsible for the accident, preferable to his brother's charges and the re-proaches of his parents. Geoffrey needs something definite to base his existence on—even if it is only the knowledge that he has killed his brother. He *must* have something firm to back up to, or he will go mad. And he feels that without his brother's presence, he could be free, careless, bold as Maurice himself. But now he will be always shrinking, coiled up like a tortoise with no shell. The thought of going through life thus coiled up within himself, morbid in self-consciousness, lonely, surly and miserable, is torture to him; he longs not to be, to extinguish himself. But Maurice does not betray him; and between the brothers an amicable affection is restored. But while Maurice is peculiarly happy, his feeling of affection swimming over everything, Geoffrey is even more alone and isolated; and he cannot bear to stand alone. Maurice is left to watch the haystack overnight; as it comes on to rain, Geoffrey returns to assist his brother, and overhears Maurice and Paula lovemaking under the stack-cloth. He feels miser-able, lonely, jealous of Maurice; and sits in the nearby shed contemplating painfully concrete jealous imaginings. Until Lydia Bredon, the tramp's wife, comes into the shed looking for her husband. She is wet through, hungry and exhausted; Geoffrey feeds her and gives her coverings. He warms her, comforts her, and she makes love to him. He is bewildered, and full of wonder. When she awakes, he feels proud to possess her: erect and unabateable; with her to complete him he feels firm and whole. He needs her, and because he needs her he loves her fervently. He wants to marry her, but she is wary, hesitant, reluctant and suspicious; but she will wait for him, to see if he will change his mind. They keep faith with one another. *Love Among the Haystacks*

WOOKEY, HENRY: Eldest son of Mr. Wookey and brother of Geoffrey and Maurice. He is a cool, crisp individual, with a cold ironical tone in his voice. *Love Among the Haystacks*

WOOKEY, MAURICE: The youngest Wookey brother: a handsome young fellow of twenty-one, careless and debonair, full of vigour. His grey eyes are bright and baffled with strong emotion; his swarthy face filled with the expectant, glad and nervous smile of a young man roused for the first time in passion. Maurice has entered a passionate liaison with Paula Jablonowsky, and his emotional disturbance is very moving to him, hardly pleasant, making him tense and brace his body with joyful pain, as his red mouth curls back and shows his teeth in a smile. He taunts his elder brother Geoffrey, who is also attracted to the Fräulein, with provocative descriptions of their love-play; and the enraged Geoffrey pushes him off the stack. On recovering consciousness, Maurice absolves his brother of guilt for the accident. Paula bends over Maurice in fierce but tender instinctive protectiveness—she cleaves to him like a mate. Maurice derives from the accident a strange new ease, an authority; new power comes to him, and he feels extraordinarily glad. He makes up his mind to marry the Fräulein. Maurice has to watch over the haystack overnight, and Paula meets him: it comes on to rain, and they have to cover the stack with a cloth. The ladder falls from Maurice's reach, and they are isolated together. In the morning, while Geoffrey is proud and contented with his discovery and possession of Lydia, Maurice and Paula are a little disillusioned, a little wan and peaky. But they become engaged, and later marry. *Love Among the Haystacks*

WOOKEY, MISS: A guest of the Tempests' at a Highclose party. *The White Peacock*

WOOKEY, MR.: A big, burly farmer, father of Geoffrey, Henry and Maurice. Red and glistening, affable and jovial, he laughs in a hearty, chaffing voice. *Love Among the Haystacks*

WRIGHT: A big, sullen boy in Ursula Brangwen's class at Brinsley Street school. *The Rainbow*

WYLD, BEATRICE: A friend of Paul Morel's, a young woman of twenty-two, small and pale, hollow-eyed, with a relentless look about her. A mocking, teasing, lively girl, who takes up with Arthur Morel. Later he marries her in an advanced state of pregnancy. *Sons and Lovers*

Y

YOUNG, DR.: A doctor at the Maternity Hospital in Islington, where Alvina Houghton works as a nurse. A plump young man of middle height, with the blue eyes of a little boy, very knowing—especially of a woman's secrets. He 'plays' with Alvina, and his touch and kiss have that nearness of a little boy's which nearly melts her. She could almost succumb. But there is an inflexible fate within her, which shapes her ends despite herself. *The Lost Girl*

Animals and Other Non-Human
Characters

ARABELLA: The child Annie Morel's doll. Paul accidentally breaks her, and purges his guilt by a ritual sacrifice of her broken body. *Sons and Lovers*

BEN, MRS. NICKIE: A black cat caught in a trap; both legs broken, she is callously but efficiently drowned by George Saxton. Her husband Mr. Nickie Ben greets her injury with indifference and masculine callousness. *The White Peacock*

BILL and LIL: Mr. Ellis's pair of greys. *The Boy in the Bush*

BISMARCK: A big black and white rabbit, whose explosions of violent fear produce a 'hellish recognition' of unspeakable intimacy between Gudrun Brangwen and Gerald Crich. *Women in Love*

COCKEREL: Bought by the peasant as a shabby little gamecock, the cockerel grows to a certain splendour, resplendent in brave feathers and arched, orange neck; calling shrilly to other cocks beyond the peasant's walls, in a world he knows nothing of. He is a saucy, flamboyant bird, never to be daunted. Fearful that he may escape, the peasant and his wife catch the cock, and tie him, struggling and fighting, by the leg. He ceases to prance and ruffle his feathers; knowing, with a gloomy foreboding, that he is tethered. But still he crows defiance to the unseen cocks. The life in him remains unbroken, although he is not free: and one morning with a great burst of energy he snaps the string, crowing a loud and splitting crow, and escapes. Recaptured, he is admired by the man who died as a bird that has risen to the Father among birds. *The Man who Died*

FOX, THE: The fox is the demon of Bailey Farm, and the

despair of its proprietors March and Banford, as he prowls secretly and furtively around the farm, casually carrying off their precious livestock. All attempts to shoot him fail: he seems to circumvent the girls deliberately. Occasionally one catches a glimpse of the white tip of his brush, or the ruddy shadow of him in the deep grass. When March encounters the fox face to face, he looks at her, and *knows* her; then makes off into the woods with slow, leaping, impudent jumps, his brush held smooth like a feather, his white buttocks twinkling. He is gone, softly, soft as the wind. To March he becomes a haunting symbol of beauty, of wonder, of maleness, of life itself. She cannot defeat him. But the fox finds his match in Henry Grenfel, a slyer and more subtle hunter than himself. In death the fox is still beautiful: his belly white and soft as snow, his wonderful black-glinted brush full and frictional. The long, fine muzzle has wonderful silver whiskers, like ice-threads, and pricked ears with hair inside; and the long spoon of the nose, to thrust forward and bite deep into the living prey. To March he is a strange, wonderful, incomprehensible, out of her range. *The Fox*

GYP: George Saxton's dog. *The White Peacock*

HUITZILOPOCHTLI ('HUMMING BIRD OF THE SOUTH'): Aztec god of war and storm-god; worshipped with human sacrifice. This divinity of feathers and serpents, war-paint and human blood-sacrifice, is one of the 'manifestations' of the old gods' return to Mexico. Cipriano finds in Huitzilopochtli the incarnation and fulfilment of his godlike self. *The Plumed Serpent*

LOOLOO: A Pekinese dog with a bulging brow, belonging to Winifred Crich. *Women in Love*

LUCY: One of the Ellis's horses. *The Boy in the Bush*

MINO: Rupert Birkin's tabby cat, superb and lordly in his domination of a fluffy grey female cat who can only submit to his 'male dignity' and 'higher understanding'. *Women in Love*

POPPY: Lou Carrington's sorrel mare. *St. Mawr*

QUETZALCOATL ('SNAKE-BIRD', 'THE PLUMED SERPENT'): The Aztec god of wind, master of life, artist, creator and civiliser;

expected to return to Mexico from the Eastern Sea. 'A fair-faced, bearded god: the wind, the breath of life, the eyes that see and are unseen, like the stars by day.' In the new cult of the god, Quetzalcoatl becomes identified with its leader, Don Ramón Carrasco. *The Plumed Serpent*

ST. MAWR: A handsome bay stallion, with ears pricked like daggers from his head; big, black, brilliant eyes with a 'sharp, questioning glint'; 'an air of tense, quiet alertness that betrays an animal that can be dangerous.' He is of a lovely red-gold colour, and a dark, invisible fire seems to come from him. To Lou Carrington he is the spirit of life itself, almost like a god 'looking at her terribly out of the everlasting dark . . . he was some splendid demon, and she must worship him.' *St. Mawr*

SINNER: A flipperty-flopperty foxhound puppy at the Marsh Farm. *The Rainbow*

STAMPEDE: A wild, unmanageable horse offered to Jack Grant with malevolent intentions by Red Easu. *The Boy in the Bush*

TAFFY: A pit-pony. *Sons and Lovers*

TANSY: A sorrel mare belonging to Mary Henrietta Urquhart, the Princess. *The Princess*

TRIP: The Saxton's bull-terrier. *The White Peacock*

The Characters — Book by Book

Aaron's Rod

The Boy in the Bush

The Boy in the Bush (cont.)

The Captain's Doll

The Daughters of the Vicar

The Fox

Kangaroo

Lady Chatterley's Lover

The Ladybird

The Lost Girl

Love Among the Haystacks

The Man who Died

The Plumed Serpent

The Plumed Serpent (cont.)

The Princess

The Prussian Officer

The Rainbow

The Rainbow (cont.)

St. Mawr

Sons and Lovers

Sons and Lovers (cont.)

The Trespasser

The Virgin and the Gipsy

The White Peacock

	Part	Chapter		Part	Chapter
Annable, Billy	II	VI	Grandmother, Meg's	II	I
Annable, Frank	I	IV	Gyp	I	VI
Annable, Jack (*see under* Annable, Mrs.*)	I	VI	May, Mrs.	I	IV
Annable, Mrs.	I	VI	Mayhew, Maud	III	V
Annable, Sam (*see under* Annable, Mrs.*)	I	VI	Mayhew, Tom	III	V
Annable, Sarah Anne (*see under* Annable, Mrs.*)	I	VI	Meg (later Saxton)	II	I
			Parrot, The	III	II
Annie	I	I	Rebecca	I	I
Bancroft, Will	I	IX	Renshaw, Arthur (*see under* Renshaw, Tom)	III	VIII
Beardsall, Cyril	I	I	Renshaw, Tom	III	VII
Beardsall, Frank	I	IV	Saxton, David	I	VIII
Beardsall, Lettice (Lettie)	I	I	Saxton, Emily	I	I
Beardsall, Mrs.	I	I	Saxton, George	I	I
Ben, Mr. and Mrs. Nickie	I	II	Saxton, Meg (*see* Meg)		
			Saxton, Mollie	I	I
Bill	II	I	Saxton, Mr.	I	I
Carlin, French (*see* Beardsall, Frank)			Saxton, Mrs.	I	I
Charles, Percival (*see under* Gall, Alice)	III	VIII	Seconde, Hilda	II	IX
			Slaighter, Hilda	II	V
Cresswell, Freddy	II	IX	Smith, Tom	I	IX
D'Arcy, Agnes	II	IX	Tempest, Leslie	I	I
Denys, Louie	II	IX	Tempest, Marie	I	VII
Gall, Alice	II	IV	Trip	II	II
			Wookey, Miss	I	VIII

The Woman who Rode Away

Indians (*see under* Lederman, Mrs.)

Lederman
Lederman, Mrs.

Women in Love

	Chapter		Chapter
Birkin, Rupert	I	Brangwen, William (Billy)	XV
Bismarck	XVIII	Crich, Basil (*see under* Crich, Thomas)	XXIV
Bradley, Miss	VIII		
Brangwen, Anna	XIV	Crich, Diana	II
Brangwen, Dora	XV	Crich, Gerald	I
Brangwen, Gudrun	I	Crich, Laura	I
Brangwen, Rosalind	XIX	Crich, Lottie (*see under* Crich, Thomas)	II
Brangwen, Ursula	I		
Brangwen, William (Will)	XIV	Crich, Mrs. (Christiana)	I

Women in Love (cont.)